MY LIFE IN STORY:

THE OUTSIDE GROOVE

MY LIFE IN STORY:

THE OUTSIDE GROOVE

Kristian Aleixo & Braxton A. Cosby

Cosby Media Productions

Cosby Media Productions ™

Entertaining the Mind, and Inspiring the Soul

My Life In Story: The Outside Groove

Published by Cosby Media Productions.
www.cosbymediaproductions.com
Editor: Toonian Pasqueralle
Cover art: Cosby Media Productions
ISBN-10: 1546573070
ISBN-13: 978-1546573074

TABLE OF CONTENTS

FOREWORD i

A WORD TO THE READER ii

PROLOGUE 1

CHAPTER 1.. 10

CHAPTER 2.. 16

CHAPTER 3.. 24

CHAPTER 4.. 31

CHAPTER 5.. 36

CHAPTER 6.. 44

CHAPTER 7.. 53

CHAPTER 8.. 60

CHAPTER 9.. 68

CHAPTER 10.. 77

CHAPTER 11.. 83

CHAPTER 12.. 90

CHAPTER 13.. 101

CHAPTER 14.. 110

CHAPTER 15.. 123

CHAPTER 16.. 131

EPILOGUE 139

SPECIAL THANKS..143

ABOUT THE AUTHOR...145

ABOUT THE AUTHOR...147

ENDORSEMENTS 149

MORE BOOKS FROM THE MY LIFE IN STORY SERIES 152

FOREWORD

It's been 17 years since I drove the world's most famous race for the second time... 17 years. In that 17 years a very small percentage of the human population has become professional racecar drivers and an even smaller amount have reached the Indianapolis 500. Only a select few can achieve what I did in '91 and '93—and I can tell you first hand, it takes a will that only a select few have, but I see it in this young man's story. He's been fearless. I've kicked open a door for the 'underdog' and I'd like to see more like Kristian step through. It won't be easy; it was never supposed to be but more than just understanding this, his mindset is of doing whatever is necessary to overcome...just like me. Over the next 200 pages or so, you will read a story not often seen (if ever) in motorsports. I hope you find inspiration in his grit and words. And to Kristian...persevere, young man. Persevere.

-Willy T. Ribbs

A WORD TO THE READER

The Outside Groove is an auto racing term used to describe the racing line closest to the wall. Because it is so close to the wall, it is often the most dangerous line. Although, on some tracks it may be the most advantageous, most drivers will choose the middle or inside because there is less risk involved. Plus, it's a whole heck of a lot easier.

Only the bold run up high in the outside groove. In many ways, my life and journey thereof, reflects that route. The path into professional motorsports is one of similar trials, banks, adjustments and turns. Speed, it seems – at least considering the rate at which one travels through life – is the most minor of all parameters to consider. The fight to compete at the highest level of racing is atypical at best. Forget anything you know about being conventional. Out there on the track, amongst other hard-nosed competitors, you find yourself pushed to the brink of virtual insanity, only to come back time and time again thirsting for more. Life is like a marathon. It's all about the long game. You take your position, hit the throttle, brake only when necessary and jockey for pole position. And just like in most races, the taste of victory is worth every painful sacrifice.

I live for it.

Die for it.

Long for the moment to take the track again.

Here is the story of my outside groove.

*— **Kristian Aleixo***

Walter B. Pitkin once famously wrote that "life begins at 40"…

That's bulls**t. Walter B. Pitkin never drove a racecar.

PROLOGUE

Man, I hate hospitals. I don't know what it is. The sitting, the waiting, the poking and prodding, all of it – I can't stand it. From the blood pressure machine that squeezes my arm just a little too tight to those ass-less gowns, going to the hospital is an unpleasantry that I'd readily trade for any number of simpler things, like licking a metal pole in the dead of winter or skydiving without a parachute. This is NOT exactly my idea of a party.

The rhythmic sound of heavy-soled shoes tapping along the white tiled floor grew louder and I braced myself for the moment that someone would enter my room. Lehigh Valley General is a labyrinth, a vast catacomb of endless hallways and numerous floors, but the layout of the emergency room is the easiest one to follow. It's got the waiting rooms outside, triage holding the east and west wings, while treatment takes place beyond the large security doors only accessible to qualified personnel. So, it's only logical that the clicking sound belongs to the person designated to give me the update on my condition. That's what I was there for, after all..

A man walked in from behind the pulled plastic curtain, holding my chart. "Well, Mr. Alexio," he said in a baritone with a raised eyebrow.

"It's Aleixo, actually," I replied, correcting him. "The 'I' is before the 'X', not after."

He smirked, adjusting his glasses on the tip of his nose. "I see." He cleared his throat. "Ahem, so it is."

"Shoot me straight, Doc. What's the damage," I asked, leaning back onto my palms and ushering him through the melodrama that might ensue. Delaying points of any kind just isn't my style; chalk it up to the racer in me. "Well," he started, lifting the front page of the chart. "You've fractured ribs three, four, five, and six right down the middle. It's not often I see a clean break like that. You're lucky it's not more serious."

"Admit it, you're impressed," I said sarcastically.

"You're fortunate to be alive," he said, more deliberate in his tone this time. "Had one of your ribs punctured a lung –"

"This night is getting rougher than one-ply," I retort. "If toilet paper were the least of your problems, I'd agree. But if we're in the business of throwing metaphors around, you might want to consider sandpaper." My eyes search the ceiling. "You know, I actually see it now. Yep, my night is thoroughly screwed."

"Mind telling me how you managed to do it?"

I shake my head and flash a smile a mile wide.

"Occupational hazard."

My mind rewinds back to just an hour prior. My hands, sheathed in reverse stitch, flame retardant gloves, reflexively gripped and released the steering wheel of the #81 car as my Crew Chief Al leaned in the door frame and barked at me with a thick Pennsylvanian accent. "Alright, bud. We drew numbers for the starting position," his voice belted above the hum of my engine. "You're rolling off P-8 tonight. Maintain the pace, hit your marks, and keep your nose clean... And above all else, don't junk my race car! I mean it, Kristian."

"I thought she was mine," I teased, pointing to my last name scribed in vinyl above the door frame.

"Just bring her back in one piece!"

I shrugged. "When have I ever junked a race car?"

When he failed to respond, I quickly added, "On second thought, don't answer that!"

He disappeared from the door like David Blaine and did his diligence of making last-minute checks on the tire condition, air pressure, and engine temperature. When he was finished, he reappeared just as fast as he vanished. "You're good, bud," he said with a thumbs up. I nod. "Cool. Hey Al!" I called just as he was leaving. "I'll sign you an autograph later!" Al rolled his eyes and tapped the hood before hiking to the top of the metal bleachers to get a better view of the track. I stared out of where the windshield would be if there were one and slipped into a trance – something like

3

a lucid dream. I put the car in neutral and added pressure on the gas pedal and the 350 horsepower engine roared to life. The digital display lights along my dashboard danced in my line of sight, the shifter begging me to fondle it and I did, giving into my cravings. My pulse quickened and I could feel the thumping in my fingertips as they wrap around the wheel and tighten. Everything around me dissipated into blackness, and the only thing that remained was the six degree banked asphalt in front of me. The car was loose as a noodle in the heat race but, with Al's tinkering of the springs, she tightened right up for the feature.

"All I have to do is pass seven cars," I thought after a quick prayer. It's the same prayer I whisper to myself before every race: "Lord, if today is my day to go, thank you for letting it be doing what I love." It was late in the summer and the humidity made the air milkshake thick. I shut the visor on my helmet like a medieval knight ready to joust and watched the condensation from my breath climb the shield. Next, I tugged the straps of my six-point safety harness until it was snug around my torso.

HANS device on, I was locked in. Couldn't move a lick. A bead of sweat that rolled down the back of my neck before being swallowed by my Nomex undershirt. I was secure in the truth of the moment and yet fearful of the utter unknown in the next. As I pulled onto the grid, on the outside of Row 4, every fan's individual face was drowned out by the stadium lights. The entire fleet of race cars began to roll forward and I'm transported to another dimension where time screeches to a near halt. Anyone who has ever experienced this can attest; you feel like Neo in The Matrix.

The routine is simple: Three slow laps under the caution flag and then green. I criss-cross my wrists on the wheel, weaving my car back and forth, side to side, to help get the Hoosier tires up to temperature. It's something I've done a hundred times over, but each second feels like the first. The heat on the rubber did its job, as the slicks hugged the blacktop with an appreciable firmness. And then... It started.

My mouth dried.

Perspiration decorated my forehead.

Green flag, hammer down!

The last thing I recall before being pinned like a thumbtack into the metal cocoon of my Butler Built race seat is the rush of cars that filled my periphery. There was an explosion of colors from sponsor decals, vinyl numbers, and advertisement banners, all illuminated by camera flashes. We played "Musical Chairs" as I jockeyed to establish a sweet spot within the draft of the leaders – you know, use the guy in front of me to punch a hole in the clean air. If done correctly, the turbulence he's driving into should whiz right over my head, lessening the wear on my engine until I'm ready to slingshot out in front of him.

We were able to pick off a few cars early on the high side but, as the groove moved gradually down the track, the window to pass up there closed quickly. Running the center line had put me where I wanted to be: P-3 and flirting with the lead. Cars darted in and out of one another behind me as the yellow flag made its first cameo of the night for the three drivers who just figure-eighted into the catch fence behind us.

Green again. About three-quarters through the race now, I ran the line near the apron, lower than snake s**t, risking a move to overtake the leader. Just as I was about to hit pay-dirt, I got brushed on my left rear tire by another driver trying to occupy the same space. The 81 fishtailed, a little but I maintained. What's he trying to do, get by me in the grass? Landscape on your own time!

Was it uncalled for? Maybe. But I can't blame him for being points-hungry. We all are. It was the 11th hour of the race and second place is prime real estate. I juiced the throttle and pressed forward, opening the gap between us. I had a bad feeling that if he got that close to me again, his front end was going to get REAL wide. I set up to make another move for the lead but he made contact... Again. This time, his car got loose and did its best impression of driving on marbles. The impact reverberated deep into my spine as I spun sideways and slid down the front stretch, out of turn four and into one. Friction brought me to a stop and I let out a heavy sigh of relief. I was safe. Or at least I thought I was.

That's when the stampede caught up with me. My eyes bolted left and right as multiple cars motored by until my vision finally locked on to a lone car barreling down the track, straight as an arrow, towards me! The yellow flag was waving but, at that speed, I doubt the driver saw it or me. BANG. Direct collision. Black swims in my head as I struggled to keep my neck from slumping.

The crowd stilled as I regained control over my eyes and scanned my surroundings. *How bad is it,* I think, as medical personnel spilled from along the fences and engaged with the mangled steel around me.

"How do you feel," a female medical staff member asked. "I'm fine. Let's get this thing turned around and finish this race," I say, somewhat annoyed at being omitted from the discussion erupting around me of how bad things look from the outside. "Tell the stewards to black flag the jerk that got into me and put me back in P-2."

"Emergency, emergency!" one man screamed into his walkie-talkie.

Sirens blared, signaling the arriving procession of two red fire trucks. That's when it occured to me: my car has caught on fire, oil spouting into the air like I had been drilling for it in Texas!

7

I was inside the car and couldn't see the damage to the outside from where I was, but heat is a little different. THAT, I could feel. A blurry tow truck came into view, trailing behind the fire engines whose hoses were drawn and pounding my car with streams of cold water. The heat subsided, and I shielded my face from the jets of water finding their way under my top-side wing.

As the flames died down and the crew dragged me from the wreck, it became irrevocably obvious that my night of racing was over. What wasn't so obvious was that shrapnel from the other car was now lodged in my torso. The pain I felt as the team laid me on a stretcher was indescribable, and medics tended to my bleeding, plugging the wound with gauze and bandages. I looked like an old teddy bear with the stuffing coming out! I peeked over to my ride and assessed the damage. "Geez, kid," Al murmured, noticing my staring.

I waved to the crowd as they cheered my survival. I couldn't help but spare a smile, celebrating that, despite my night being over, I'll live to drive another day. "You still want that autograph, Al," I joke.

Al ignored me, eyes on my gash, with a face of concern that piqued my own interest. A male physician leaned in over me. "How are you feeling now?"

I answered the only way I know how. "Like I got drilled by a car at 100 miles an hour." I winced behind my grin. "Adrenaline only goes so far, Doc…"

8

And I blacked out from the pain.

Hours later, I awoke, eyes on the ceiling of my hospital room, with the faint scent of pine floor polish lingering in the air. I felt my side where my wounds were replaced by staples and a mesh film covering. I hopped down off the side of the hospital bed and lifted the side of my ass-less gown to get a better look at the reflection of my battle scar in the mirror. Just another day at the office. "Man, I hate hospitals."

CHAPTER 1

My mother was born in Madeira, Portugal. She moved around a bunch with my nomadic grandfather, a talented painter who dabbled in the art of sculpting. Aside from being a transient artist, he boxed professionally in Europe before bouncing from Portugal to several islands in the Caribbean. Their mainstay was Antigua, though, because of its significant Afro-Portuguese community.

His athletic genes didn't miss my mother as she excelled in both track and field, winning several medals in high school and college before later migrating to United States.

My parents met at a birthday party held at Club Leviticus in my father's hometown of New York City, hosted by the great Bobby Hunter of the Harlem Globetrotters. Hours into the affair, women from wall to wall, my father was still fixated on one that he spotted earlier, telling anyone who would listen about her natural elegance and beauty. He had just enough time to introduce himself to her before her friends came and snatched her away. He was overcome with a curiosity that wouldn't quell itself until later that evening, when Bobby Hunter arrived with good news.

"Hey man, I got someone I'd like you to meet," he said. As coincidence would have it, the woman he wanted to introduce to my father was the same one he'd been babbling about all night – my mother.

"Nice to see you again," my father said, shaking the woman's delicate hand with a smile broad enough to reach each ear.

"Same to you," she replied with a head nod.

"Uh...I take it you two have met," Bobby asked, slightly puzzled. They laughed and filled the rest of their evening agenda with dancing and getting better acquainted.

Closer to midnight, my father's good friend Gus Williams – former NBA champion with the Seattle Super Sonics – turned up and remembered to pass on a message. A coach who was holding an open tryout for an Emerald City semi-professional basketball team had reached out to him in search of prospective players. "I may have dropped your name," Gus said. My dad had been cut from an NBA practice squad a few years prior but thought he still may have had something left in the tank.

"Come on, what do you have to lose," Gus asked. "You're a natural athlete and, of course, you'll have to make a few adjustments, but I wouldn't tell you if I didn't think you had a shot of making it."

"Okay, fine," my father said finally, refusing to allow Gus' pitch to drag on any longer and take away another minute of his time with Mom. A few weeks later, Gus explained how the process would work and the idea quickly infested the minds of both of my parents. My mother was swept up in a tornado of hope that my father would someday make it to The League. I mean, who wouldn't be? Trading in the average day-to-day life of a newly emigrant woman for a few seasons of fast-paced NBA action, or maybe even going overseas to watch my dad hoop, was inviting. He made his best last-ditch effort to play ball in Seattle and that's where it all changed: the woman he'd met at a party in The Big Apple was pregnant.

My mother told me that she always knew my father wasn't the "settle down, solo woman'" type of guy. The idea of marriage never really took root and was more of a faint whisper in his mind. She knew his commitment level was on the lower end of the spectrum, so she never tried to convince him otherwise. In her words, "He just is how he is," and she accepted the arduous task of being a single mom and raising a rambunctious little boy on her own.

It was September 23rd, typically the first day of fall, when I came into the world. Life was kind enough to present me with a challenge on my very first day. Not only did my mother's water break at just five and a half months in, I was upside down in the womb! What can I say? I'm a rebel. After being in labor for a few hours shy of a full day, the decision was made to perform a C-section and cut me out. I was little more than palm-sized, being born 4 months early and all, and the doctors informed my parents that I was never going to grow to a normal size. That's when I was taught my first lesson in life. Medical degree or not, don't ever let anyone tell you what you can't do. Here I stand at 5 feet 11 and a half inches tall and 160 pounds. I fought, but the struggles to stay alive from that premature age persisted. I'm told that I died several times – in the clinical sense – in the incubator which served as my home for the better third of the next year. When I finally convinced everyone that I wanted to do this whole "being alive" thing, they allowed me to leave.

As a young child with a single mother, I was often left in the care of my grandmother, her mom. She would come to visit for extended periods of time and, on more than one occasion, pinched my cheeks so hard that I swore she'd given me permanent dimples. One of my earliest memories as a child came from my Avo (Grandma in Portuguese). Every visit was Christmas as far as she was concerned and, when you answered the door, you could barely see her curly brown hair over all the gifts she was cradling. One time she brought me a Washington Redskins helmet and jersey. Clearly she wasn't a football fan because she didn't realize that the Redskins play in Washington D.C. and not Washington State! I'm a Seahawks supporter but, looking back on it now, I couldn't be mad. It's the gesture that resonates with me most. That helmet and jersey got lost somewhere in the shuffle of moving houses but it's definitely something I wish I held onto, as my Avo died a short while after the move from brain cancer.

I was only five years old when she passed and couldn't truly grasp what happened. I only knew that I had never seen my mother so sad. She'd lost her best friend, and you don't just rebound from something like that. Trust me, I would know – but we'll get to that a bit later.

My mother spiraled into a depression and, for fear of me seeing her at her worst, sent me to Los Angeles to visit my paternal grandmother for the summer. That brings me to my second earliest memory. I was visiting Disneyland for the first time and went for a ride on the back of a live elephant. The elephant was trained to loop us around the entire park. It was supposed to return you to the starting point where your family would be waiting for you, but my elephant decided to go rogue. He thought that scaring the living daylights out of a five-year-old sounded like a lot more fun and broke course, wandering off. At first, I panicked like any five-year-old would, and began wailing as if someone had thrown hot water on me! I vividly remember wondering what would happen if the elephant did not return me and if I'd ever see my family again. When the initial shock wore off and my tears dried in the California sun, I felt strangely calm. Somehow I knew that even if that elephant never brought me back, I would still be fine. Maybe I'd read *The Jungle Book* one too many times but, in my mind, I would find a way to make it my friend.

Shortly after the elephant's wayward romp, a trainer wrangled it in and led us back to my grandma who, by then, was in hysterics. To this day, she still doesn't understand why I was smiling!

CHAPTER 2

I was back in Seattle by the close of summer and it wasn't long after starting kindergarten that my mother was diagnosed with Type 1 diabetes. Interestingly enough, prior to her diagnosis, there was no family history of the disease. She did her best to keep her illness clandestine, dealing with the fight in secret. She never explained to me what it was or how it worked, so I never really had much concern for it. But I guess that was her point. She'd drop 10 to 20 pounds in what seemed like 10 to 20 days and, when I'd point out the physical changes like the rapid weight loss, she'd say it was because she wasn't that hungry. Always a naturally thin woman, her runner's physique had withered to a brittle 95 pounds.

My formative years were spent as close to a mother as a son could be. As a boy, the wallpaper in my room wore the design of a luminescent blue sky, complete with marshmallow-like clouds of various shapes and sizes. Every night, not a second past 7:30, my mother would detour on her way to her room at the end of our long hallway and duck into mine. Oftentimes, she'd lie next to me and we'd stare at those clouds until my eyelids became as heavy as bricks. She challenged me to find fresh shapes and figures among them. I'd share the same ideas night after night but she never shot me down, she'd just encouraged me to upgrade my finds to something a little more daring. "Instead of a cat, why don't we try a lynx or a Siberian tiger tonight," she'd say.

Above the quintessential mom duties like the train of soup and cold rags she brought me the time I got scarlet fever, she allowed me to make mistakes. You'd get only one warning in that house and, if you persisted, she'd trust Karma to teach the impending lesson. I mean, she wouldn't let me leap off of a cliff or juggle with knives, but I was allowed to test the elasticity of safety on smaller levels to see how far it would stretch. All truths told, I learned better that way – through experience. The golf ball-sized knots on my head from jumping on the bed one more time than I should have or the front teeth I lost from doing the same on the living room couch (after being warned not to) were all necessary. I'm thankful she didn't raise me to be a safe little boy; I don't think they get very far. I always had a license to be dangerous, one I wielded rather loosely, so when she'd play triage nurse and patch up every scrape and laceration, I was appreciative. In saying this, please do not think that I didn't have any discipline. There were plenty of times where the proverbial whip had to be cracked. I'll never forget the time I asked her if I could go to the park and play and she told me not until I showed her that I could tie my shoes correctly. Until that day, I had only done so with her assistance and now it was my turn to fly solo. I must have done it 100 times if I did it once, but the final product was still deemed "too sloppy." Was she serious? I'm missing valuable time on the swings here! "You're going to get this right. No son of mine is going onto that playground with loose bunny ears for laces," she said.

At the time, I didn't care what my laces looked like. I just wanted to go out and play, but she was having none of that. Didn't budge an inch. With protesting growing increasingly futile, I caved and did it her way. I laced so many times that day that I swore I could do it blindfolded with one arm behind my back but, by the time it passed inspection, it was too dark to go out. Needless to say, I was upset. I howled like a banshee and stomped my way to my room like I was making wine, declaring how unfair she was. I couldn't appreciate it at the time but this was her way of instilling in me a sense of pride in my work and the satisfaction of a job well done. No matter how long it takes. Two lessons I'm extremely thankful for now.

I was enrolled in a Catholic elementary school, which meant that slacks, button down shirts, ties, cardigans and penny loafers were my daily attire. I looked like a miniature Carlton Banks from Fresh Prince of Bel-Air! School was never my jam, which led me to be disruptive in class. If I wasn't cracking jokes, playing with the hair of the girl in front of me, or firing off spitballs from a plastic straw like a howitzer, I was daydreaming or falling asleep. Looking back, I just didn't see the point of the classroom setting. It wasn't that I didn't enjoy learning, but the process was too structured for a wild one like me. I'd rather do it on my own terms, preferably outside in the natural world versus having the natural world explained to me on a chalkboard. I hardly completed any assignments for lack of interest, but what kept my head above water were my outstanding test scores.

It was all a game to me. How far could I go without putting forth a true effort? How much could I not pay attention in class, read the lesson on my own and still get the highest grade? These personal challenges made school less mundane and kept me intrigued. In a weird sort of way, I took pride in being the only kid in detention with a 95 on the latest quiz. The only thing I credited my ability to perform well on tests to was all the knowledge I was soaking up at home. Being an only child meant that I had to entertain myself and create my own fun, so I frequently lost myself in my encyclopedia collection. I would bring a pillow and blanket into the bathroom, lock myself in and pretend that the dry tub was a capsule that could transport me anywhere, as far as my imagination would let it. I'd sit there for hours and just absorb everything I could. From astronomy to myth and folklore and geography to history. In doing so, I picked up what we learned in class plus so much more that they wouldn't have even taught us for another year.

But school stories aren't what I remember most about this age. What sticks out in my mind is my relationship, or lack thereof, with my father. I'm sure it isn't uncommon to hear of similar stories from other children who grew up in a single-parent home, but that's what stands out the most to me. Partially because my father and I still have a broken relationship to this day, the impact is still present now. A lot of the decisions I've made about how to live my life were an attempt to get as far away from him and his example as humanly possible. Although I'm sure there had to be some good times peppered in there somewhere, there were far more when I felt unwanted and unimportant. Far more times when I felt like I wasn't made a priority and was too blind to see that. I must have looked like a fool. My mother would always say "Your father is on the phone" in a sarcastic tone and my naivety wouldn't allow me to digest what she was saying or why she'd say it that way. I'd just get excited, as any kid would be for the chance to talk to the man who's supposed to be the hero in their life.

When I did talk to him, we'd go through all the formalities. You know, how was school and how was your day, but I'd always arrive at the inevitable question. "So, Pop, when am I going to see you?" There was always a long dramatic pause and then, "Uh, how about this weekend? We'll go shoot hoops or ride bikes, or we'll toss the ol' pigskin around." I'd be stoked all week and tell anyone who made eye contact – teachers, friends, mom and the mailman – how my dad and I were going to do all this cool stuff. Friday afternoons I would run home as fast as my legs would carry me to pack my things in anticipation for the big weekend. My mother would get home late in the afternoon from work and ask me what I was doing with my duffle bags filled to the brim sitting by the door. "Waiting for my dad," I'd reply confidently, recounting all the amazing things we were supposed to do over the next two days.

She just shook her head and said "I don't want you to get your hopes up." "I'm sure he is on his way right now," I'd say as if the apocalypse itself couldn't stop him from seeing me. "You'll see. He'll be here."

She smiled half-heartedly. "I'm not saying he's not coming, but your father has a way of disappointing people."

"Well, you're going to be so wrong this time when he knocks on THAT door," I'd say, pausing to look at the brass knob attached. "Annnny minute now," I nodded smugly.

And so I waited... I always waited.

I remember making a basketball hoop out of an old shoe box and hanging it above the inside of the door frame in my room. I would shoot a ball made of tin foil into it just to pass the time. "Aleixo fakes left, then right and shoots the three," I'd narrate, pretending to be my dad on the court. Swish! "And the crowd goes wild," I'd shout in my best Marv Albert impression. Eventually, I'd fall asleep on top of my bags and wake up the next morning to my mother carrying me to my

21

bed. I stayed optimistic that he would show despite his absence that day. I clung to the remote chance over the next few weekends — "He'll be here, he has to be. He loves me." My optimism extended months and then years, but he never came. I still struggle to forgive myself now for believing in him for so long. I really must have looked like a fool.

My father's absence meant that I had to find other outlets to express masculinity, as well as try to identify solid examples of what a man should be. Ironically, considering how fabricated I know it to be today, I turned to professional wrestling. I became completely obsessed with the WWE. Guys like Shawn Michaels, Bret Hart, The Rock, and Steve Austin became my surrogate fathers while my dad's unwillingness to change only ensured that there wouldn't be any reconciliation between my parents.

Sometimes I think this may have actually been the best case scenario. At least I didn't have to go through the classic "my parents are getting a divorce" drama that so many of my friends were experiencing at the time. I had never even known my parents as a couple. The son of two athletes, sports became a refuge for me during my elementary school years. It was something to fill the void my dad left, and it didn't hurt that I excelled at them. Not to stroke my own ego here, but I played everything at a high level. Baseball, basketball, football and, after seeing Disney's *Mighty Ducks* movies, even street hockey – everything. My favorite, though, was running. It was something that connected my mother and me. She used to say, "God gave you a hard head and my feet." It was at school track meets that I had my first taste of speed – albeit on foot – and I was hooked.

Cutting through the wind like a javelin and watching the finish line speed towards me as I thrust forward towards it was magical. If my chicken legs could go any faster, I'd probably take off like a 747! The idea that no one could touch me made me feel invincible. For me, speed equals freedom, and free I was. Little did I know at the time how true that statement would become.

CHAPTER 3

Towards the end of the 6th grade, my mother's health began to take a sharp nose dive. For the life of me, I can't explain what she was going through mentally at the time but, for some reason, she decided to stop taking her prescribed insulin.

"Why won't you take your medicine," I recall asking her for the umpteenth time. After blowing me off, she finally provided me with an answer that left me zero comfort. "It's the needle. It hurts and I'm tired of hurting myself," she said, her eyes welling with tears. "You wouldn't understand."

I would often wake up in the middle of the night to find her asleep on the couch, her pajamas pulled halfway down her thigh (the target site), and a full syringe dangling from her index and middle fingers, evidence that she hadn't taken her medicine again. To make matters worse, she would consistently eat all the wrong things: sugar-laden foods that made her glucose spike like a stock market chart to near fatal levels, greatly increasing her risk for amputation, heart attacks, and strokes. After being hospitalized more times than I'd care to count, she was eventually relegated to a wheelchair and could not use her legs for long periods of time due to poor circulation. That's when I realized that the situation was far more critical than she'd let on.

Most of my nights were split between taking care of her and trying to keep up with homework that had taken an even further backseat to her condition. I remember feelings of intense anger swelling within, all directed at her. Not because I had to take care of her – Lord knows I owed her for all the times she took care of me – but because she was letting diabetes win. To me, my mother had always been the strongest woman on the planet. Now here she was in a wheelchair, crippled by depression and giving up. I guess even Supergirl has her Kryptonite.

I was angry because I believe there should be no lengths a parent wouldn't go to stick around as long as possible for their children. That means doing WHATEVER it is that you have to do, no excuses. Whether that's denying your sweet tooth to manage your sugar intake or injecting yourself 4 times a day to maintain your glucose levels, even if it hurts sometimes.

On weekend nights, we would curl up on our cozy gray couch under the wool blanket that my Avo made for Mom when she was little and watch horror movies together because she was afraid to watch them alone. "I want this forever." I remember thinking. "Doesn't she want this too? Why won't she do what the doctors told her to do? Why doesn't she care enough?"

25

Living out of a wheelchair made her incapable of performing her duties at work as a court clerk, so she was forced to vacate her position. With less money coming in and no help from my shadow of a father, we had no choice but to move out of our well-to-do neighborhood in Seattle and go 40 minutes south to significantly more urban Tacoma. This also meant that I could no longer attend my private academy and would have to join the ranks of the Pierce County public school system for junior high. It was like moving from Sesame Street to New Jack City! I was in a state of complete discomfort. A new city and a new school meant I was forced to make new friends – well, at least try to make new friends. I was riddled with the usual preteen insecurities of not knowing if I had anything in common with the other kids. It turned out that I didn't and I became an instant social pariah.

Rap music was forbidden at my house, so I had never even heard a full song until that point. I can remember the first day of 7th grade when I was asked who my favorite rapper and song was. I didn't have an answer and racked my brain trying to muster up a name that sounded remotely familiar. A simple question that sparked an immediate headache. "I like the Fresh Prince," I said, warranting a low chuckle from the amassing crowd. "Ok," the lead antagonist said. His name was Terry Jordan, recreation football All-Star and kid-legend in Tacoma. "What other kind of music do you like?" The pressure in my head expanded like air in a tire. My fingertips went numb as the crowd around me became fuzzy, leaving only Terry in my view. "Do you know Billy Joel?"

Crickets.

"Billy who," Terry bellowed mockingly at me. So I carried on, desperately trying to find some common ground. "Er...Elton John, Smokey Robinson, Prince...?" I pressed on, every attempt failing worse than the last. The entire schoolyard erupted in a laughing tizzy.

"Well, THAT went well," I mumbled, rolling my eyes. Junior High: 1, Kristian: 0.

To add to it, public schools have a pretty lax dress code. I had been wearing a uniform my entire academic career, so my personal style mirrored my school attire. That made me the only kid in slacks, a button down, and cardigan, while everyone else was rocking baggy jeans and a fresh pair of Air Forces. I was teased about this relentlessly and physically picked on because of it. I would constantly get into fights because someone would try to take my tie and play a round of Keep Away or something stupid like that. I'd like to say the experience of attending school was becoming less and less enjoyable by the day, but that would be an understatement. It was more like by the minute! When I woke up every morning, I knew with a degree of certainty that, at some point during the day, I would have to fight. It became so regular that I probably could have scheduled it into my

27

itinerary. I wondered where all the nice kids were. There had to be some at every school... Right? I considered getting some new gear to fit in, but my mom was on a spandex-tight budget and couldn't afford it. So I fought, physically and mentally, to keep my composure. It hardened me and made me less affected by people's opinions of me. In hindsight, Terry Jordan and his flunkies created a monster, because now I fight for my dreams every day. It also didn't help that my test scores were still excellent. Nobody likes the smart guy and they were sure to let me know it. It's just not the popular thing to be at that age.

The only source of encouragement at this stage came in the form of a girl named Victoria. She had moved into the house next to mine and man, I fell hard. Silky, raven hair and eyes greener than the state of Washington itself; I was "sprung." No, whatever comes after sprung. That's what I was! I found myself going out of my way trying to impress her. I wrote poetry, sent flowers, bought candy, you name it. When I found out her older brother raced soap box derby cars, I hatched my latest scheme to win her over. I found an encyclopedia book at the library and studied as much as I could on how to build one. The plan was to win the next race and then she'd have to fall in love with me. I mean, girls love winners, so I was determined to perfect the skills required to be one. I worked on my rust bucket like a mad scientist for several weeks. It was an eyesore at best, but I was still very proud of my hard work. It was built with no supervision or help, out of old shopping cart parts and other junk yard gems. Unfortunately, but not surprisingly, it was about as fast as it looked and I lost the race. Any little interest I had in racing quickly evaporated, only to have the racing bug repay me a visit four years later (and you already know how that turned out).

Over the winter of that same year, my maternal grandfather randomly surfaced. Suitcases in hand and intentions to stay in our house, he settled in and made himself comfortable. My grandfather was a strange man, more of a mythical caricature than an actual person. The majority of my limited interactions with him were via the occasional long distance call. We'd never talk long because it would run up the phone bill. Until then, I had never physically seen him, so I was skeptically thankful for this cameo in my life. He became a sort of stand-in father at a time when I desperately needed one.

He was short and stocky - a typical boxer build - with an extraordinary gift for art. He was tougher than a $2 steak and didn't allow me to get away with a quarter of the things I wanted to. Laziness and a lack of discipline were thought to make a young boy soft and would not be tolerated in his presence. In essence, he was my first drill sergeant long before I enlisted in the U.S. Army years later, and he would sometimes lay hands on me if the punishment fit the crime. I hated him with a fevered passion in the moment but, in hindsight, his brand of no-nonsense was exactly what the situation called for. It gave me direction.

The following year, my mother corralled all the strength she could to come watch me graduate from Junior High. I had never seen her as proud of me as she was that day. We took a picture of a congratulatory embrace that I still struggle to look at now. It took all she had to wheel her chair down to the stage and stand up to hug me. That version of her, the one in the photo – frail, with eyes sunk in and legs trembling because they hadn't been used, is all I can see whenever I look at it. Junior high was just steps behind me, high school just steps in front of me, and I wasn't prepared for what happened during the winter break of my freshman year.

CHAPTER 4

I entered high school with a different approach. I was on a mission. After receiving the real-world education that I couldn't get in private school and not wanting to put up Rocky Balboa-worthy performances every day for the next four years, I used my birthday money to purchase some new threads that helped me blend in. New kicks, flashy jeans, and a Seattle Mariners hat tilted to the side. And you know what? It actually worked.

The bullying stopped completely when I joined the junior varsity football team as a walk-on. Sharp reflexes, velcro-like hands, and an ability to change directions on a dime made me a shoo-in to play wide receiver, but it was my speed that made me dangerous. I gained popularity as an athlete and thought I'd use the leverage to make up for the last 2 years. One night I dragged myself home from practice – pads on my shoulders, fresh grass stains on my pants, and my helmet still in hand – to find my dad at my place. Nobody had called him – hell, I hadn't so much as uttered his name in weeks. He was just... there.

"What's up, Dad" I asked.

"Nothing, son. Aren't you going to come and greet your old man like a man? Aren't you happy to see me?" He stood there, arms wide open, as if I owed him something.

After exchanging the usual pleasantries, I retreated to my room as he and my mom sat on the living room couch for what seemed like long enough to leave permanent silhouettes in the cushions. I hugged my ear to the door in my best attempt at eavesdropping on their conversation. It was a failed effort, barely audible and resembling the spotty reception of an old radio with no antenna. I was only able to steal away segments of a talk that centered on life, death, and the future of the world, *my* world to be exact. What all that meant in the moment, I had no clue but, in recent years, my dad has disclosed the details of their hushed dialogue that night.

See, that was the night my mother told him she felt like she didn't have much time left. She told him that she'd be dead soon. I don't know how she knew but my guess is when you're that sick, you can sense it. Not-so-funny thing was, she was right.

***

On December 22nd, just as school was letting out for winter recess, I came out to the living room to check in on her and ask what she wanted for dinner. Often lethargic because of the diabetes, it was no surprise to find her on the couch napping. "Mom, wake up, it's time for dinner," I said. "God, she's a heavy sleeper." I tapped her shoulder, gently at first, and when she failed to respond, I nudged her again. My nudge gradually grew to vigorous shaking as panic set in. If my teeth chattered any harder, they'd shatter like icicles.

"Mom, WAKE UP," I shouted, my voice shrill with fear. You know that one scene in Lion King where Mufasa has fallen from the cliff only to be found by Simba seconds later? Yeah, totally me, right now. Her mouth parted and her eyes rolled back in their sockets before closing. I raced to the phone. I can still hear the monotone beeps as my right index finger mashed each digit. Nine-one-one. I went catatonic. What snapped me out of my hypnosis was the faint wail of sirens and the screech of ambulance tires rounding my corner. Within moments, a sea of navy blue Pierce County First Responder shirts poured through our front door like a tidal wave. They managed to pry her eyes open as she came to.

"Ma'am, what is your name? Do you know where you are?" The EMT asked her.

She shook her head slightly and answered, but her words were slurred so badly that everything sounded like she had stuffed her mouth with cotton.

"Her name is Madeleina, Madaleina Aleixo" I interrupted, hoping that hearing her name would arouse her from her disorient.

"Ms. Aleixo, who is the President of the United States?"

"Carter," She replied. Carter? Jimmy Carter hadn't been president since she first moved to America. "Ms. Aleixo, what month is it," he asked, flashing a light across her eyes. "May," she answered confidently, and with all of the fresh powdered snow still atop our window sill. None of it was making any sense and my level of worry was rising.

"We're going to take her in, kid," the EMT said, gripping my shoulder. "Everything's going to be alright." I began to breathe easier. He's a trained professional and if he says she's going to fine, I best believe him. They loaded all 95 pounds of her onto a stretcher and peeled off into the night. We arrived at the hospital and she was immediately rushed into the ICU with her blood sugar so high that the glucose meter couldn't give a reading! After a few hours of the physicians attaching leads and tubes to her limp frame, she was upgraded to stable condition and my grandfather and I took a very silent ride home.

The next day my father came to visit and announced he'd be staying with us until my mother was released. Yay. My heart fluttered with sarcastic joy. I wasn't sure how I was supposed to feel about that. Days passed and the absence of my mother at home made the tension between me and my dad wind up like an old alarm clock. And, as predictable as the movement of the hands on a clock, one evening emotions bubbled over and an argument ensued.

"Turn that video game off and get to your homework," he said, leaning his head into my room.

"Man, you got no reason to be giving me orders," I replied.

"Excuse me," he said.

I stood, the PlayStation controller clutched tight in my grasp. "You heard me. Now you want to stroll in here making rules like you've been here for years. You're not the boss of me!"

He pointed at me like a laser. "I'm going to let that slide because I know you're going through a lot with your mother being in the hospital, but you better calm down RIGHT NOW."

"Or what," I challenged.

He took a step towards me, positioning himself nose to nose. "Or I'll show you I mean business."

There was something alien in his voice, an octave out of him I had never heard before. Although it shook me like a pair of dice, I refused to cower. I never backed down from the older kids who took my tie and I didn't see the point in starting now! The air was polluted with tension. Silence, staring, ice in my eyes, jaw clenched, nostrils flared and, most importantly, no visible signs of the tremors inside.

"Whatever," I said finally, turning away and sitting on the edge of my bed. He cut the television off and exited my room. That's when I lost it and slung the controller at the nearest wall, chipping the sky pattern wallpaper my mother and I spent so much time looking at. I didn't have a strategy for what to do next. But the rage inside of me sparked a Plan B: leave!

CHAPTER 5

I packed a bag and took all of the Christmas money out of the cards my aunt and cousins had sent – something that totaled 50 bucks – and left. Save for summer camp, I had never been away from home before. Without a clear-cut destination in mind, I headed to the first place that felt the most like home: Tacoma General and my mom.

I spent the rest of that first evening watching her sleep under heavy sedation until the visiting hours for minors were over. The security guard, "Officer Hard-Ass" as I liked to call him, made it clear as water that 9 P.M. meant 9 P.M. and I had to go. I pecked mom on the forehead and "hopped" the bus back home. Sorry Bus Driver, but I only had $46 left to my name and I wasn't trying to spend it on Pierce County Transit!

I arrived home still angry at my dad and itching to prove a point. I didn't need him or his rules, I thought. But, I did need a place to stay, so instead of knocking on the door and admitting defeat by sleeping in my own bed, I queued the *Mission Impossible* theme music in my head and stealthily climbed the rain gutters in the backyard to the attic. Dark, freezing, wet, and dusty, it was no Hilton, but angst-filled teen logic said sleeping amidst a few cobwebs was better than going back inside.

I camped out, jumping at every creak of the wood and perceived footstep I heard until the next morning. Around 6 A.M., when I was sure my Pops and Grandfather were still asleep, I made my way to the kitchen to raid the fridge for a snack without anyone noticing. With my stomach full, it was back to the attic to spend the better chunk of the day reading the latest wrestling magazines and stuffing my face with the Skippy peanut butter and crackers that I swiped from downstairs. When the sun set, I returned to the hospital and dashed into the gift shop just as they were shutting the doors an hour early for the Christmas holiday.

"What'll it be, young man?" asked the cherry-cheeked cashier in a candy cane striped dress.

"Let's see, how much cash do I have left," I thought, fumbling through my pockets and removing a wad of crumpled bills.

"Um... the roses, the teddy bear, and that 'I heart mom' card over there please," I said with slight hesitation, not knowing what the total would be.

"$44.60" flashed across the register.

Whew, I had just enough to cover the tab.

I gathered my things and waited for the ding of the elevator. It was Christmas, and I didn't want Mom to miss out on the one day of the year where everyone should be joyful. When I got to her room, surprisingly, she was already awake and talking...kinda.

Her voice was so weak and airy that I had to lean in close to make out her words. "How you doing, kiddo?" she asked.

I swept her hair to one side of her face. "I'm good Mom. You know you don't have to ever worry about me. You just worry about getting out of here," I replied.

"I know I don't have to worry about you, Filho (son in Portuguese). So strong. Don't you ever lose that."

We talked and laughed until the security officer reminded me what time it was. With visiting hours now over, I leaned in as close as I could, the bed's guardrail digging into my abdomen, and gave her a kiss on the cheek. "I love you, mom."

Her smile crowded her eyes. "I love you too, Filho."

"Oh, I almost forgot. Merry Christmas," I said as I reluctantly shut the door behind me.

This.

This right here. This right here was the last conversation I would ever have with my mother. The doctors said she slipped into a coma early the next morning on the 26th. All of my friends awoke that day, eager to play with their new presents. Me? I was too busy losing the best gift I ever had.

The frigid breeze of that morning left frost streaked across the glass, but it barely matched the bite of the cold in the attic. I slept there anyway because my adolescent pride would rather me turn into a popsicle than to ask my father's forgiveness for running away. I tip-toed my normal route to the kitchen cupboard when I got hungry but was caught mid-forage. Much to my surprise, HE apologized to ME! My stubbornness faded and I was allowed back inside. The next morning, we all sat in the living room together – me, my father, and my Grandpa. Grandpa was doing a crossword puzzle and I was helping. "Hmmm...What's a 7-letter word for –"

The cordless phone rang, breaking my concentration and my dad answered it.

"Good morning. Hi, Dr. Lee."

Grandpa looked up from the page and stared at me, grim faced. "She's dead," he whispered.

"No, they're probably just calling to give us an update," I said, shrugging off his macabre sentiments.

With the phone pressed to his ear, dad nodded slowly in agreement of whatever Dr. Lee was saying. "Mmm-hmm, mmm-hmm, I understand." With a *click*, he hung up the phone. "Son..."

"Hey, what's a 7-letter word for –"

He cut me off. "She's gone."

December 27th, I lost my best friend. The world as I knew it crumbled. I didn't know what else to do, so I ran. I grabbed my jacket and ran. I flew out of the door, my feet almost coming out of my shoes. The wind sailed past my eyes and dried my tears along my cheeks. My breath escaped me but I continued planting one foot in front of the other until my legs gave out and I collapsed on the gray cement. As I lay on my back, the morning sky filled my eyes, slightly blurred from my crying. It was overcast, but all I saw was my wallpaper. And that's where my father and grandfather caught up with me. Lying on the ground, sobbing. They picked me up and slid me into the back seat of Mom's Ford Tempo, the one she affectionately named "Rosie" after her mother and drove to the hospital. Drunk with sadness, I stumbled through the sliding glass doors and we took the elevator to the basement. That's where the morgue was. There she was. It was true.

My everything.

My horror movie buddy.

He was the one who taught me to tie my shoes, how to whistle, blow a gum bubble, and color inside (and sometimes outside) the lines, was gone.

***

School was to resume shortly and the funeral was slated for the following weekend. There was no way I was even close to being ready to be back at my desk. I toyed with the idea of just not showing up until I could get my head screwed on straight, but my father thought otherwise.

"It would be better if you had something to take your mind off of your mother during the day," he said, leaning against the door jamb of my room. Standing there with his arms folded, he almost seemed to make sense. So 6 days after my mother's death, there I was.

Needless to say, I was NOT in a good place emotionally and it caused me to behave out of character. I remember being at my locker when my good friend Andre came up to me. He had been one of the few kids who befriended me since junior high. I can't recall exactly what he said at the time, just the gist, but I got angry for what must have felt like no reason at all. I exploded on him. "Knock it off, alright," I screamed with an edge to my words.

"What gives with you man," Andre asked. "All I wanted to know is if you were going to hang out after school or if your mother wanted you home early."

He didn't know of my mother's passing because I hadn't told anyone, nor did he say anything to warrant my next response. I cocked my fist back and put it square on his chin! Andre keeled over, holding his nose. I had never hit anyone in the face before and his eyes watered just the way I imagined someone's would if they were sucker-punched unexpectedly. I didn't feel good about it one bit, but the swing purged the anger within. I reached my hand out to pick him up from the floor but he wrenched himself away and scurried off. As I watched him hurry away, I felt myself slipping into a place where I just wanted to hurt something. Losing my mom at this age was unfair and I wanted others to feel the pain I was feeling.

Days later, I caught up with him by his locker and apologized. "Are we 'boys' again?"

"Yeah, we're cool. You didn't hit me *that* hard," he said as the corners of his mouth turned upwards before extending his hand for our secret shake.

That snowy Saturday morning, the day of the funeral, I had beaten the sun out of bed. Hell, I hadn't been to sleep at all. It wasn't for a lack of trying; I just couldn't close my eyes without seeing my mom's. They were mine too, the same ones she gave me. My dad peeked in. "Oh, you're already up? Can you be dressed in an hour?"

I nodded silently, my gaze fixed on the wallpaper. I've never been keen on wearing suits, but I wanted to look my best for her. As I stood in the long mirror wrestling with the Windsor knot my dad never taught me to tie, it hit me like a Mack truck. This was real. Like, really real. I had talked myself into thinking that she was on some kind of vacation or maybe still at the hospital and I'd just go visit her tomorrow.

That dream faded like the color on a favorite t-shirt as we walked through the cemetery. It was a typical service, except that it was MY mom in the casket. I had somehow managed to remain stoic and unemotional the whole day until then. Peering down into the six foot deep hole, there was no denying that she was never coming back. In that instant, reality knocked me on my ass and I lost it. I begged, pleaded, for the undertaker to open the casket.

"Please, you have to let me see her one more time. You just have to!" Desperation was sketched on my face.

"You know they can't do that," Grandpa said.

As they lowered her into the ground, I think just about every tear I ever had in me left my body. The Pastor said a few closing words and as people shed from the grave site, I remained kneeling in the fresh snow. My father stood some distance behind me and I recognized his voice amongst the crowd of departing visitors. "Come on, Kristian. It's time to go."

CHAPTER 6

For the remainder of the school year, my family put the "fun" in dysfunctional. I had no choice but to move in with my dad and his then-new bride. This was obviously a decision made out of necessity rather than preference. Absolutely nothing about the situation was ideal, and that's looking at it through rose-colored glasses. If I had it my way, I would have opted to stay with my grandfather in the house I was already in, but being stationary never fits well into a vagrant's plans, does it? He disappeared just about as soon as the funeral ended and we haven't seen him since. Living with my father and a new stepmother who was trying entirely too hard to replace my birth one made for constant arguments. He had rules, she had rules, and I wasn't interested in either. How could I be subservient to a man I had very little respect for and his practically still-a-stranger wife?

When I would reach my limits and get frustrated beyond what I could handle, my best friend Jacob and I would take our skateboards to the biggest hill Tacoma could serve up. It started on 48th Street and ended at Pacific Avenue. We would go to the top, sit on our boards and race each other to the bottom – well, as close to the bottom as we could get. Neither of us ever made it all the way down, which was probably a good thing with all the traffic waiting for us at the intersection below. We never made it all the way down because by the time you got past the second hill, the speed was too much for your plank. Your board would rock side to side like a sailboat in a category 5 hurricane and you'd wipe out, hard! Totally worth it. I can't tell you how many good pairs of pants were shredded to confetti up there, but it didn't matter. I was free.

Speed has a funny way of forcing you to be in the moment. It makes it so that you can't think of anything else. It demands all of your attention and commands your entire body. And if you go fast enough, the sensation overrides rationality and the danger of being seriously hurt.

Back at school, I was dealing with a lot and behaving more and more out of character. Eventually, I did something I'm not too proud of and briefly joined a gang for about all of three days before summer recess. I was the "smart one" of the crew and quickly realized it wasn't for me when the other gang members started asking me for help with their homework. Uh...no thanks guys, I don't even like doing my own!

That summer, I developed a major crush on a girl. I mean, I was *Jonesin'*. Her name was Daria and she lived in a yellow house with white shutters across the way from my step-mom's pad. I had spoken to her once or twice in the hall at school after 7th period Spanish class, but chickened out on the chance to ask her out. Somehow, through the "Gossip Girls Network" that every school has, her older sister Fannie found out how I felt and decided to hook us up. I still remember that awkward conversation like it was 10 minutes ago. I was in my yard when Daria and her sister came over to greet me.

"So how's your summer going," Fannie asked.

"It's cool," I replied, humoring the small talk and trying to smother my anxiousness. Fannie must have sensed it and bypassed the malarkey, getting straight to the point. "Do you like Daria?"

The goose bumps along the back of my neck came alive and crawled down my spine.

"I don't know," I said, shrugging and trying not to look at Daria. "Why would you ask that?"

Daria whipped her neck like a snake. "Quit playin'," she replied.

"I ain't playin'. I'm serious!" Fannie's eyes centered on me like the scope of a hunting rifle. "You know you look at my sister funny."

Daria stood next to Fannie, fidgeting with the fringes of her sun dress.

My eyes dropped to the ground as my mind raced for a snappy comeback to throw her off my scent. But I came up empty.

"Well," she prodded.

"Stop," I said finally, looking Into Daria's pupils and seeing she shared my level of discomfort.

"You're making us both uncomfortable," Daria added.

"What? You two should hang out," Fannie said, her eyes beading back and forth between the two of us. "He's not ugly!"

"I never said he was ugly," Daria exclaimed.

"So why don't you go out," Fannie asked, hands now on her hips. "Because he's not your usual type?"

"What's that supposed to mean," Daria questioned.

The same query filled my mind. Did she have a type? And how come I wasn't it?

"You know you like them thug types," Fannie said with a Cheshire cat grin. She winked at Daria and then turned her attention back to me. "You 'bout that thug life, Kristian, like them dudes from LA?" I vaguely recalled some story of Daria dating a gang leader at our school. Granted, it lasted one month, but that still gave me no insight as to why. Daria was sweet, cute and smart. Why any girl like her would go for a punk like that was beyond me. I shook my head in anticipation of how she would respond.

Fannie looked me over as if she was trying to figure out a complex algebra equation.

"That may not be such a bad thing, you know, because those roughnecks will get you nowhere," she said.

"You know Gabriel and I broke up," Daria retorted, swatting at Fannie.

"So it's settled. You two will hang out," Fannie declared. "Are you free right now?"

"Like, single," I asked.

"No, like free. Now," Fannie pressed.

My hands found my pockets.

"Yeah, I guess."

The entire scene was suffocating, so I decided to change the atmosphere, literally. "Daria, would you like to go for a walk?"

"OK."

We did a lot of walking that summer and, nine times out of ten, we'd end up at the waterfront near Ruston Way overlooking the Puget Sound. Our conversations mainly hovered over the next phase of our lives after high school and my mom.

One time, Daria taught me a valuable life lesson that hasn't left my mind yet.

As we sat on the waterfront, watching the tug boats vanish over the horizon and into the sunset, she leaned on my shoulder. I was suddenly overcome with courage and lifted her chin with my index finger. I lost myself in those big brown eyes and asked the question that had been rattling around in my brain for weeks.

"Can I kiss you?"

You know that scene in the movies where everyone's having a good time at a party, someone says something off-color, and the DJ scratches the record?

"I know this is new for you, but you don't ask a girl if you can kiss her." She poked me in the chest. "You've got to be a man about it and just go for it."

And so I did, pressing my lips on hers as softly as I could. My first real kiss lasted for a little over three seconds. I'm not even sure how I got home that night but I swear I flew there because I never remembered my feet touching the ground. That was an awesome summer, one I needed after the year I was having.

Daria and I rejoined our respective social castes for sophomore year but every time we'd pass each other in the hallway, we'd share a smile. She helped me through a very difficult time in my life and I was grateful, but everything wasn't kittens and rainbows just yet. I had just begun to improve at school when things at home became dire. A side note to all the ladies reading this book: if a man is trifling in one situation and does not desire to change, be prepared to be Bill Murray in *Groundhog Day*. Whatever my father's MO was with my mother had resurfaced in his new relationship and, just like my mom, she wasn't having it either. She kicked him out.

His getting the boot this time didn't just affect him this time; with no mom to turn to, I had to roll with him. He found us a room to rent in the back of someone's house but, without a steady job and a long deflated basketball dream, he couldn't keep up with the payments and, after a month and a half, we were back to the drawing board. What do you do when you've got a kid to take care of on your own now and NBA ambitions don't pay bills? His solution: a storage unit in a warehouse. Locker number 4313 was only $19.95 a month and that's where we slept. Embarrassed and ashamed, I didn't know of any other kids in school who were homeless, and I did my best to keep that tidbit of news to myself. Now that the amount of effort I was putting into my class assignments was on an upswing. I had to maintain my newfound motivation to get away from a 5x7 slab of cement surrounded by a chain link fence, meant for packed boxes. I mean, the lights go out at 8, so all tasks that require little things like vision had to be done prior. I couldn't drink water after 5 either because there was a big sign in bold crimson letters that "strictly prohibited human occupancy after business hours," and I'd trip an alarm if I got up in the middle of the night to use the bathroom. A hornet's nest of cops sniffing around our spot and thinking we broke in was the last thing I needed. Those few days I spent in the attic as a "runaway" were starting to look like Club Med now.

I got by with a third of my homework missing on the strength of my test scores. Thank God for my bread-and-butter! By the end of the year, I had so much pent-up anger and rage that my fuse was getting shorter than it had ever been. I might as well have been walking around with "TNT" branded on my forehead. One day in art class, I dropped my pencil and it rolled close to another student's foot: Jimmy Lyle. He picked it up and smirked at me.

"Pass it back, man," I had asked, obviously not in a playful mood.

"What do I look like, your mother," Jimmy said.

The four walls around us went hazy and before I could gain control of my hands, they had balled into fists at my side and barreled out of control on a collision course with Jimmy's face.

I was alone and lost and, just like Andre the year before, he became a bystander to my rage. Unlike Andre though, Jimmy snapped back like a rubber band and landed a few blows of his own, dazing me for a second. I stumbled backwards over my own feet. You can tell I watched way too much pro wrestling by what I did next. I picked up the nearest folding chair and swung for the center field wall. Jimmy's heels left the marble-tiled floor of our classroom and didn't meet it again until his back hit the ground. I crashed the chair down on his head. Thud. Again... And again... Seconds later, I was surrounded. A dozen hands grabbed hold of me and I blacked out. When I awoke, I was in the principal's office awaiting my sentence.

Jimmy didn't know that I had lost my mother and his harmless sarcasm did not excuse my behavior but, for me, it was simply the wrong thing to say at the wrong time. It's not one of my finer moments. I'm not perfect by any means and I don't condone my actions, but in the interest of keeping this book "real" it was a story I had to tell. I was a kid dealing with some pretty heavy issues and I was ill-equipped to handle them all by myself and all of the time. Despite my father's pleas to the Principal, the Department of Education charged me with "use of a weapon" and I was suspended indefinitely and ultimately expelled.

In retrospect, this wasn't entirely a bad thing. The time off from school was what I needed to begin with following my mom's death – to heal. It allowed me time for reflection, time to rethink life and find perspective. I contemplated everything, most importantly who I wanted to be. The possibility of transferring to a new school would give me the opportunity to be that guy. I could cut ties with all the anger and start fresh.

I gave my dad a short list of prospective schools in our district, ones I could see myself thriving in. I felt like a pro sports star entering free agency! I didn't have to wait long as my #1 choice obliged. With as much anticipation as I had for school in forever, I was ready for the fall. I was back, baby!

CHAPTER 7

My grandfather had two '67 Volkswagen Beetles that he bought for pennies during his stay with us. One eggshell white, one Easter blue, but only the blue one would turn over when you cranked the key. Sure, she'd sputter a bit, cough, wheeze, and bellow some smoke first, but if you asked her nicely and told her she was pretty, she'd fire up. I visited the shed where it was being kept by a family friend and decided to give her an end-of-summer makeover. I was like John Travolta in that "Grease Lightning" scene, minus the hair gel and leather jacket. In no time, my hooptie was more than drivable; she was halfway to being a bona fide hot rod!

The early mornings and even later nights put into revitalizing her also gave me something to distract myself from not having a decent place to lay my head.

It was September now and on my very first day at the new school, I dropped my car key while leaving Social Studies. I was so focused on note taking that I didn't notice the chime when it hit the ground. A girl named Jasmine saw it and chased me down.

"Excuse me," she said, tapping me on my shoulder. "Did you drop this?" She held out the key with the huge 'VW' carved into its center like a Halloween pumpkin.

"Yes, actually." I took it from her hand. "Thanks."

She was a freckle-faced cutie and I was liking this school already.

"Can I give you a ride home? I mean, it's the least I can do for you since you saved me the walk back to my place."

She shrugged casually. "Sure."

After way too short of a ride to Tacoma's North End, I crept up her folk's driveway and slammed the car into park.

"So you live here?"

"Mmm-hmm."

The idea of living in a house again one day, maybe even one as nice as hers, made me feel warm.

"Well, here you are," I said, swept up in my daydream.

"You're sweet," she said with a smile before leaning over and stamping a kiss on my cheek. "It's just a house, Kristian. See you tomorrow."

"Maybe for you it is." I thought. "Maybe because you've always had one." But I think I'll keep my big secret to myself.

Two things: 1. I was never washing this cheek again, and 2. I needed a roof over my head that didn't come with a padlock and a rolling gate.

The year was starting off great. My new school was a much needed reprieve from the last. No fighting every day. No fights at all, actually. I was accepted, enjoying moderate popularity and, with the exception of my living arrangements, happy. One Friday night, I was invited to a classmate's birthday party and while I was there, I was introduced to a long-haired guy named Steven. Steven headed up a small club at our school for import cars. Most of the kids had Hondas – Civics, CRXs and Preludes galore – but since my Beetle was German made, he counted it as an import and invited me to join.

"What do you say, man? You in?"

"So it's like a gang, but for guys who like cars," I said, rubbing my chin. I glanced over at my ride as the edges of my mouth curled.

"You ever heard of Gymkhana?"

"Jim who," I replied.

Steven shook his head.

"No, Gymkhana. It's something like autocross," he continued. "I could tell you about it, but if you come with me tomorrow morning, I'll show you."

The next day, Steven sent a mysterious, one line text message, containing only the address of where we were to meet. 11 A.M. was the prescribed time. When I arrived at the coordinates, there were orange traffic cones set up in a football field-sized parking lot, their various configurations creating makeshift driving courses. Steven outstretched his arms toward the cones, inviting my eyes to take in its splendor. "This, my Beetle driving friend, is where it all goes down," he said, an air of pride trailing his statement.

"Where what goes down?" My heart skipped so fast you'd think it was playing double-dutch.

"Racing, man," Steven said. "Run-what-you-brung style. Competing cars are separated into classes. Rear wheel drive, front-wheel drive, and all-wheel drive, as well as by horsepower to keep things even. The rules are simple. For every cone you hit, one second gets added to your time. Fastest through the cones wins."

This began my affair with auto racing. There was no Vin Diesel in sight but, I was about to star in my own Fast and the Furious.

"You want in," Steven asked.

I nodded slowly. "Hell yeah."

The coolest thing about autocross, in my opinion, is that literally anyone can participate with any car. You don't need to have some souped-up machine to make the grid. All you need is a lemon and some heart and I had both!

I spent all of my weekends junior year competing. There was something so pure about the simplicity of it all that would slap a smile on my face for days and, by the time that smile started to wane, it was the weekend again and time to hit the track.

The Beetle was a museum relic. She was slow as tree sap and handled like the RMS Titanic, but every now and again, when she wanted to, and if the cones were configured just right, we'd put down a good lap time together. Sometimes the throttle would stick.

Sometimes I'd have to triple pump the brakes to get her to stop, but once I fastened the chin strap on my helmet, she became much more than my grandfather's jalopy. I wasn't going to win any trophies, not even for best looking car, but I was living it up and that's all that mattered to me – to feel like that kid on a skateboard at the top of a hill again.

I zigzagged in and out of those cones all the way until senior year when I got my first job. My school gave fourth-year students the option of attending class during the day or working and attending class at night. I chose the latter and found employment as an office assistant at another high school – mostly making coffee and copies. Although my housing situation had somewhat improved when my dad wormed his way back in with my step-mom, my plan was to save enough money to escape once and for all.

One of the bright spots that year was my math teacher, Mr. Sackeyfio, a spectacled intellectual from Nigeria with an accent thicker than sludge, who we affectionately nicknamed "Sack." Sack was 20% math teacher and 80% philosopher. The first 15 minutes of class would touch on numbers and equations, while the next 45 centered on life and making the most of it. He understood the journey into the real world and wanted to prepare us for lessons that math couldn't teach. We soaked it up like mops.

I remember one time, Sack had noticed my eyes were fixated on a young lady in class. When the bell rang, he pulled me to the side.

"Kristian, can I see you for a moment," he asked.

"Sure, Sack, what's up?"

He waited for everyone to file out and closed the door behind them.

"What is your plan to win that girl?"

My cheeks burned. "What girl?"

He wagged his finger at me. "Don't try to hide it from me, boy. I know that look in a man's eyes. It's hunger!"

I told him that I had no plans and that I was going to keep my mouth shut.

He held his peace...until the next class, that is. Throughout the hour, he started hinting to the girl that someone in the room had it bad for her.

"Lauren, someone here thinks you are very beautiful."

10 minutes later:

"Lauren, I know someone here who would like to take you on a date!"

If I could have died right then, I would have. Even though no one was on to who he was referring to, I felt exposed.

At period's end, I went to confront Sack.

"Um...What do you think you're doing?"

"You mustn't be afraid, Kristian. Fear should be faced, especially when it stands in the way of getting the things you want. So you'd better get a move on because I'm not going to stop here. Each day my hints are going to hit closer to home until you tell her how you feel."

"Are you serious," I asked, eyebrows raised to the ceiling.

"Look at this face, Kristian. Sack does not joke," he replied.

"Relax. You don't have to marry this girl, but you do need to man up and tell her that you think she's beautiful. Remember, no risk, no reward," he said, pressing his finger into my chest, just over my heart.

The next day, I took his advice, not that he left me much choice. I mustered up the backbone to stop by her locker and divulge how I felt. It was all I could do to stop Sack from exposing me to the entire student body. I saw her from a distance and closed in as she was dialing in her combination. When I got there, the door hinges screeched open, revealing a picture of some guy taped to the inside wall. It turned out that she already had a boyfriend at a different school. Was I bummed? Sure. But that wasn't the point. The point was that my fear didn't turn me to mush. I told Sack what happened and he said he was more confident in me than ever. Hell, I was more confident in me than ever! I was dangerous.

CHAPTER 8

It came time for the final math exam. Math was always my worst subject and for all my test taking prowess, I tanked this one. I failed it by two questions that I left blank. So close... but close only counts when throwing hand grenades, and close wasn't going to stop Sack from pasting a fat red F on my paper. However, when I got my final grade, it had mysteriously been changed to barely passing. Curiosity made me ask Sack about this on the final day of school.

"Something interesting happened," I said.

"Oh yeah," he replied.

"Yeah. There were these two trigonometry questions that gave me fits on your final and I left them blank."

"Kristian," he started, placing his chalk caked hands atop my shoulders. "Your potential is too great for the four walls of this classroom and I am excited to see what you can do out there." He pointed out the wood-framed window. "Those two questions weren't any more important than that."

I hugged him and tried desperately to fight the tears threatening to make their escape from my eyes, but it was too late. The weight of the gesture was too heavy. A man that I respected believed in me.

Fast forward 7 days and I was standing atop a stage, wearing a royal blue cap and gown with gold trim – same as the rest of the graduating class. I had done it. I had done it from the confines of a 5x7 storage unit. I had done it on 2 meals a day. I had done it with no electricity after 8 P.M.. I had done it with no place to do laundry. I had done it having to shower in the school's locker room. I had done it without my mom and, although she wasn't there to wheel her chair down to the front row this time, she still had the best seat in the house: my heart. I HAD DONE IT.

As the summer wound down, I had a very serious decision to make. What was I going to do with my life? College? Join the working force? Who knew? Then one day, the light bulb above my head flickered.

My dad and step-mom were going at it again. Shocking, I know. These two don't just push your buttons, they break them – and I was maxed out on tolerance. I had to go and I had to go now. The quickest escape hatch I could think of was to join the military. Green is my favorite color, so I decided the Army was the way to go. I wish I could say I joined for nobler reasons but the truth is, I was running away. Not to the attic this time, but to independence and hoping to have a little adventure along the way. No pun intended, but I marched into my recruiter's office and John Hancocked the enlistment papers. It wasn't meant to be a career path or a permanent fix, just an exit sign above the door of everything I had known until now. My destination was unknown but "unknown" had to be better than here!

I didn't tell anyone what I had done because I knew they'd try to talk me out of it and, frankly, for all they put me through, I didn't owe anyone an explanation. A week later, I took the Armed Services Vocational Aptitude Battery, or ASVAB. It's an exhausting test, comprised of 10 sections. It takes about 4 hours and is used to measure your general and special intelligence. Your scores from the word knowledge, paragraph comprehension, arithmetic reasoning, and mathematics knowledge part are tallied and dictate if you meet the basic standards. The other six, ranging from science to auto mechanics, determine what you are best suited for.

I slammed my pencil down like a post touchdown football the second I was finished and anxiously awaited my results. "I'm not going to have any fingernails left when this is done. It's all good though. No pressure. It's not like my WHOLE military career is riding on this one test or anything," I thought sarcastically.

In the break room, the other recruits and I paced frantically, enough to spark a fire on the carpet with our tennis shoes if we wanted to. We discussed the areas where we felt we could have done better. I, of course, was stressing over the math part.

My recruiter came through the door, winked and motioned with his head for me to follow him.

At the time, the Army offered 213 jobs and with my "Go-go gadget test taking" ability, I qualified for damn near every one of them! It was time to pick a military occupational specialty. As I sat there in my Army of One t-shirt, carefully combing over each page of MOs and their descriptions, I had a feeling that mine would choose me and not the other way around; I'll know it when I see it. And then… "74 Delta - Chemical, biological, radiological and nuclear specialist. Responsible for defending the country against the threat of CBRN weapons and weapons of mass destruction." Those words danced on the page like Baryshnikov.

"Holy s***, I'm going to be a badass!"

When I told my recruiter, he asked me to reconsider.

"The position is very dangerous."

"Yeah…and," I quipped back. That all but sealed it for me.

Unbeknownst to me, it is the unwritten duty of the recruiter not to necessarily give you the position you requested, but to try to steer you towards what the Army is short on at the moment. It wasn't until he found a crack in my armor that I would entertain other ideas. He dangled a carrot in the form of a $15,000 signing bonus to become an 88 November- Logistics and Movement Control Specialist. For a guy who wasn't too far removed from being homeless, I didn't need much convincing.

I returned home to tell my folks and chose to break the news to them during a game of Wheel of Fortune. We all sat in silence until the show was over. When the credits rolled by, my dad got off the couch to hug me and tell me he was proud.

"I wish you would have told me what you were planning, son," he said, his eyes glossing over.

"We both do," my stepmother added. "But the question I have is why?"

Why? WHY? Hmph...

"Because I can't live this life anymore. I have to make my own way."

My eyes found their way to my father.

"Be my own man."

And with that sentence, in that instant...I was one.

It wasn't long after that my overhead was stored, my carry-on was in my lap, and the rest of my luggage was stowed away in the belly of an airplane bound for basic training.

Fort Jackson, South Carolina should be nice this time of year – at least that's what my recruiter said like some kind of travel agent. 6 hours in and I was the farthest east I had ever been. When the plane landed and the hatch sprung open, I took one step out and the sun stripped the words "Damn, it's hot!" right out of my mouth.

South Carolina at the beginning of September is no joke. I was used to sub 80-degree temps and a perpetual rainy mist and they threw me into what felt like the Middle East already. I was corralled into a van with seven other newbies from all over the U.S. and shuttled to base. Upon our arrival, we were asked to take everything out of our bags and dump it on a gray painted floor. A young man in uniform walked around our individual piles, scrutinizing every item and plucking just about everything that could be used to have an inkling of fun out of them – cell phones, iPods, and PSPs. He and a few other soldiers tossed it all into a big trash bag.

"This is all contraband and you won't see it again until the end of training," he said. "Welcome to the US Army, Hooah!" He smirked as he walked out of the door with our belongings.

"Douche," I whispered under my breath, my former life as an unruly teen begging to resurrect itself.

I was suddenly overcome with uncertainty. Had I made the right decision? If I didn't, it didn't matter; it was too late to turn back now. We were issued a gray army sweat suit with black combat boots and told that this would be our uniform until we made it out of the reception phase. Reception was like Army Purgatory; you have to wait for the training cycle in front of you to graduate before you can start and, depending on when you get into town, it can take up to 10 weeks to make it out. I was regaled with horror stories from guys who got there just as a cycle was beginning and had to stay there that long. Basic training is already lengthy and you don't want to stay any longer than you have to. I lucked out and only had to be there for one week(?).

During that week, I was given a classic buzz cut by a barber (I use that term loosely) who didn't care about your edges or hair line. He was here just to get the hair off your head and did it with the finesse of an elephant on roller blades. I was also given the Army handbook and told to memorize the ranks, the Army Creed and my personal favorite, the Warrior Ethos. I'll always place the mission first. I will never accept defeat. I will never quit. I will never leave a fallen comrade.

You know that one scene in The Wizard of Oz where Dorothy tells her dog they're not in Kansas anymore? Well, change "Kansas" to "Tacoma" and call me Toto!

It was a Tuesday, the day to start basic training and the first time I put on a real uniform. I buttoned my camouflage top and did a double take at my reflection in the mirror. "Aleixo" stitched above one breast pocket, "US Army" above the other.

Whoa, that's me!

When we pulled into the training site, deep within the Fort Jackson compound, the action started immediately. We poured off of the bus and were told to stand in a line and wait until we were assigned a letter from A through C. Every trio spouted off A, B, or C until everyone had a letter. We were then ordered to write our assigned letter on the bottom of our duffle bags and for everyone with an A to go here, everyone with a B go here, and everyone with a C go there, without delay.

Everyone scrambled to get their bags to their designated area and then after about 30 seconds, we were told to freeze. If you had your bags in the correct place you had to "beat your face:" hit the dirt and do push-ups to the tune of 10, 20, 30, 100 – whatever number you were up to when the drill sergeant got bored of looking at your pitiful mug struggle to keep going.

"If you were strong enough to lug all of your own bags by yourself, why didn't you go back and help the others you saw dragging theirs," he snorted.

Deep. I get it now. It was one of many lessons aimed at teamwork and, as we kept doing push-ups until everyone's bags were in the correct pile, I learned something. It's not about me. It's about how or where I can help the next man or woman. "ALWAYS GO BACK" was the motto. From there, with our arms still barely attached, we were christened the 3rd platoon Mad Dawgs.

CHAPTER 9

We were soon properly introduced to our three drill sergeants: Air Assault combat veteran Reese, Army Ranger hopeful Sims, and female rookie Hodges. We were then told to go around the room and introduce ourselves by name and hometown. It didn't take long to realize that those who were from stereotypically "tough" cities got it the worst. If you hailed from New York, Detroit, Chicago, or LA, you and push-ups became close friends. Thankful for me, the Pacific Northwest doesn't carry much of a rep.

The next few weeks were physically and mentally taxing, but it helped that I didn't have the added strife of being homesick like everyone else. I hated – no, I loathed home, so working for my own money and not having to worry about my dad fouling up made me relish every millisecond away. Others weren't so resilient. Jeremy Honaker, the biggest bible thumper from Missouri and a good buddy of mine, started to show cracks one morning. Around 3 A.M., in the darkness of our sleeping bay, he crept into the latrine and rammed a pencil up his nose in an attempt to pierce his brain. He wanted to die. He yelped, waking me just in time to see him fall to his knees in agony, the blood spewing from his nostrils like a water main break. I shouted for help and when the medics came to cart him off, I handed them his glasses and Bible. He was fortunate to have survived but for obvious reasons, was discharged and sent home.

I was never quite able to sleep the same after that. Everyone kind of resumed their day-to-day but, because I was closest to him, it bit me the hardest. I decided to make good use of my insomnia by enterprising Fire Guard and CQ duties. Both are done for two hour shifts each night and who it falls on goes in alphabetical order. The fire guard on duty would have to sweep and mop the floor, as well as do a bed check each half hour to make sure all soldiers were in their bunks before waking the next guy up for his two hour stint. CQ was 120 minutes of standing at parade-rest outside of the front desk and signing people in and out of the building. Typically, guys didn't want to get up in the middle of the night for their turn, and I couldn't blame them, so I hustled. For 20 bucks cash in hand and no IOUs, I'd pull your shift for you. I made a killing trying to become the Steve Jobs of 3rd platoon. Drill sergeant Reese caught on eventually when he saw me at the CQ desk for the 4th night in row.

"Back at 'A' again, huh," he grunted with suspicion as he looked me up and down.

"Well...I...uh..." My brain couldn't conjure an excuse fast enough.

"I don't know exactly what it is you're doing, but I know I'm not supposed to let you do it," he said in his raspy Texas drawl. I explained my moonlighting.

"Ballsy. Reminds me of something I would have done back in my day."

Reese was a talker. He shared countless stories of how he'd bent some rules and broken others during his time in the Army. He even recounted the time he was demoted from Sergeant First Class for slugging a Captain at a bar who "stared at his ex-wife just a little too long." Some nights, he'd whittle his own Air Assault rappelling rope and vent to me about the broken relationship between him and his daughter. We got a lot closer than we should have as drill sergeant and Private, but I made sure not to ever let it affect my professionalism. I maintained my respect for him, even when it was just the two of us. He was actually a lot cooler than he was in the daytime (mainly because he wasn't making me beat my face!) and had a lot of life experience to draw from.

The rest of basic training saw me go through the gas chamber where every ounce of fluid in my body exited through my nose, learn how to fire an M16 A2 rifle, earn a "Sharpshooter" badge, and score an "Expert" grenade-throwing merit to boot. I'd just shoot them into the foxholes like one of my dad's mid-range jumpers. Swish!

Week 9 was "survival week" at the Valley Forge obstacle course. We slept in the forest and endured surprise mock attacks under the cover of the canopied trees. The drill sergeants would wake you up by popping a can of CS gas near your tent and then lighting you up with dummy rounds as you ran away if you didn't get the lead out of your pants. Sure, these were "Hollywood" rounds, but they still stung like wasps!

Days later, with the welts still healing and bruises turning every color of a mood ring, I added marching onto the graduation field at Fort Jackson to my life's highlight reel. When I set out, I wasn't sure what to expect, but I met every challenge and won. I looked at the crowds of family members who had come to support their sons, daughters, brothers, and sisters, but no one came for me. It was in that moment that I realized I had won my freedom from my past, as well.

The following eight weeks were spent at Advanced Individual Training in the fishing Town of Newport News, Virginia. Fort Eustis, to be exact, was where I learned to be an excellent logistician and movement controller. Budding leadership skills had me eventually walk out of those post gates with the rank of Specialist.

From there, the Army gave me a couple of weeks off to max and relax. I rode the train back to Tacoma to check on my folks. Walking the streets of my hometown with my freshly-starched Class A dress uniform, I was beaming with pride. So many people stopped to shake my hand, pat me on the back and applaud what I was doing. Where was I headed? My old high school, to visit the man who put the battery in my back. I didn't mean to disrupt Mr. Sackeyfio's class, but the second I entered his room, he stopped what he was doing and swallowed me up in a bear hug.

"You did what you set out to do. What I knew you could do," he said to me, teary-eyed and crushing me in his arms. "If only your mother could see you now." If only.

The Army has what's called a " Dream sheet," and they weren't kidding when they named it that. It's supposed to be your top three choices of where you'd like to be placed for permanent duty. I chose Hawaii, Germany, and Italy. I can only imagine the person in administration who received my request laughing his head off because I got sent where the Army needed me, not where I wanted to go for summer vacation. The Grand Canyon State: Arizona. The weather wasn't much of an adjustment from South Carolina. The air was a hell of a lot drier, but it was good practice for what was ultimately next: Iraq.

I remember that day vividly, in HD and surround sound. About a year in, the logistics fellas and I were lounging in the motor pool, playing cards in our down time. I was just about to lay down a sweet pair of aces when Master Sergeant Brown came in and everyone scattered from the table like ants, pretending to be busy.

"You turds aren't fooling anyone! Take a seat," he said, glaring at the table full of cards folded face down.

"I want to talk to you all about the war in Iraq. As most of you know, I served in Kosovo, North Africa, Bosnia, and Desert Storm. I can smell when my troops are about to get their hands dirty. May not be today, tomorrow, or six months from now, but just know that the Logistics Corps is vital in the field and, because of that, I'm damn sure THIS unit will be getting the call."

There was a pregnant pause as we digested the information.

"Didn't scare any of ya, did I?"

The room was so quiet you could hear a lady bug piss on cotton.

"Didn't think so. Carry on," Master Sergeant Brown said, a scent of bravado hanging from his words.

He exited and we stared at one another with blank expressions until someone sat back at the table and began reshuffling the deck.

I couldn't speak for anyone else, but fear had filled my lungs, making it difficult to breathe. Not the frozen kind of fear that a deer experiences from an oncoming car, the excited kind – like when you're waiting in line for a rollercoaster. I don't have a logical explanation for what I did next other than that license to be dangerous – you know, the same one my mother gave me when I lost my two front teeth – had been collecting dust. I needed something to wake me up and adrenaline lasts longer than coffee. I had something to prove to myself.

My spit-shined leather boots found their way to Master Sergeant Brown's office, where he was meeting with our Lieutenant. I stood outside at parade rest, biting my bottom lip, anxiously waiting to be called in.

"Come in, Specialist," he said. "You here to quit?"

"No, Big Sarge. Quite the opposite."

They shot a glance at one another.

"Spill it," said the Lieutenant.

I swallowed.

"I don't want to wait until our unit gets called, sir. I want to volunteer to go now."

The Lieutenant leaned forward across the desk, narrowing his eyes to examine mine.

"Are you sure this is what you want," Brown said, tapping on his commemorative mug with "Desert Storm Veteran" on the front.

"I'm sure. One thing about me, Sarge, is that I can talk myself into anything."

"I don't know if this makes you brave or stupid," quipped Brown.

"OK. Let me make a few calls and see if I can get you out," remarked the Lieutenant as he exited the room, shutting the door behind him.

I smirked at Big Sarge. "Stupid."

I was in luck. A movement control team was being mobilized in a few weeks. 48 hours later, I was called back into the office and handed my orders. It was real now. I didn't know how to tell my family or the girl that I was casually dating. You can't just plug that into a casual conversation. "Oh by the way, I'm going to war for a year. How's your salad?"

While trying to figure out the best way to break it to them, I realized that no one would ever understand my reason for volunteering and that I'd have to deal with everyone's questions, comments and critiques.

So, I lied. They'd take it a whole lot easier if they thought the Army was ordering me to go. It would make everything a lot easier on me too.

The day in-theater training began, I was as "green" as the grass. All I had known of war until that point, I had seen in movies. Those were movies, though, and it was easy for my mind to separate a script from reality. But the thing is, those movie scenes were someone's reality. This isn't a bunch of kids chasing each other in the backyard yelling "bang bang!" with finger guns. Every day, I was a little less naïve than the day before, especially on the days when we'd do combat training. We'd game plan for engaging the enemy, both from a distance and in close quarters with bayonets, knives and hand-to-hand. It was like wait, my job is movement control! Why am I learning how to sack a house with hostiles in it? It's because out there, it doesn't matter what your job is. Out there, if under attack, everyone is in the infantry.

CHAPTER 10

The unit I was attached to was extremely small, and even that may be an overstatement, especially by military numbers. Most units had at least 150 to 200 soldiers; however, were a group of only 12. A dirty dozen. The grueling days of training eventually turned into lonely nights and moments spent staring at the cracks in the ceiling realizing that you may have just signed your own death warrant.

Watching the steady number of American soldiers killed in action spike on CNN makes you wonder if and when your face would be the next to flash on the TV screen. I wasn't the only one who was worried, though. A friend – well, she was a little more than a friend – was having similar thoughts. Her name was Sidney James, and she was a "single" mom from Allentown, Pennsylvania. I'll explain why I used quotation marks in a minute.

Sidney also volunteered, but with a different motivation. She had dollar signs in her eyes when she caught wind of all the tax-free income we'd make while deployed and thought her daughter could use the bump in her college fund. We promised to help each other get through the tour. Our unit of 12 was assigned a Captain as our commanding officer. She was Diane Johnson - a Desert Storm vet who assured us that we were "in good hands" so many times that she might as well have been an Allstate commercial!

The first leg of the journey was from the U.S. to Germany. The girls in our unit grossly over packed and didn't want to carry their luggage, so a couple of the fellas and I took the liberty of helping load everything onto the plane. Before boarding, and after seeing what we had done, our pilot rewarded us by upgrading our tickets to first class while the ladies had to stay in coach. "This whole war thing might not be so bad," I thought with my hands interlocked behind my head and my legs extended.

A flight that seemed long enough to get us to the moon eventually found a runway in Stuttgart. The 8-hour layover was just enough time to sample the finest schnitzel, kraut and bratwurst the airport had to offer. Note to readers: don't refer to bratwurst as "the really big hot dogs;" the locals will know you're American right away!

With our bellies stuffed, the mission pressed onward to Kuwait. The next airplane we chartered was a lot smaller and definitely military grade. No frills, no first class, and the seats only came in one variety: "hard-as-s***." I dozed off for the first time during the trip in the lightly air-conditioned cabin and awoke to a static-y "This is your captain speaking. Welcome to Kuwait" blaring over the loudspeaker directly above my head.

The hairs on my arms jumped like leap frogs from my skin with eager anticipation.

"Let's move, team," Captain Johnson shouted as she led the charge out. The hatch opened and I got my first taste of the Middle Eastern sun, or should I say it got its first taste of me. It felt like a sauna, if that sauna was inside of an oven, and that oven was in hell. A couple of Corporals who had already been on the ground for a couple of months greeted us with hearty laughs. "Did I miss the joke," I thought.

One stopped and slung his M4 carbine over his shoulder.

"You've been in-country for 30 seconds and you're already dripping in sweat?"

"Fresh meat," his buddy said, slapping his back in jest as they walked away. Jerks.

We were transported to an area just off of the airstrip while Captain Johnson ventured in search of our sleeping quarters. Camp Arafjan was a sprawling flatland of sand covered buildings, lush palm trees, and light shrubbery. A few people in our unit went to explore and I hung back because someone had to watch our bags. Sidney stayed behind too, but for a different reason. She was having a conversation with one of the soldiers who unloaded our gear. I couldn't hear exactly what she was saying but, with her arms flailing in the air, I could tell the discussion was intense. A little too intense for a first-time encounter. She stormed off like a derecho shortly after and I sparked a conversation with one of her close friends who filled me in.

"What gives," I asked. "That's Sydney's fiancé," she said with an eye roll, bummed to be giving me the bad news. "He doesn't know that they broke up. She stopped answering his calls and mailed him back the engagement ring, but he must not have gotten it because, well, he's out here."

"Well, I guess they have a lot to talk about," I replied mildly.

***

Captain Johnson returned with the rest of our team a couple of hours later with word that she had found our new "home" – a warehouse on the north side of base. Everyone and everything was accounted for, except for Sidney. When asked if I knew her whereabouts, I tried to cover for her and said she wasn't feeling well and went to find a bathroom. In reality, she still hadn't returned from the talk with her fiancé.

We delayed as long as we possibly could before heading out. Sometime later that night, Sidney caught back up with us and the brass dug into her like wet soil. It was looking like we'd have a new President by the time the lecturing about accountability and its importance during wartime ended, and I felt embarrassed for her. We shared that warehouse with two very large units and literally hundreds of people had a front row seat to her personal life. As a punishment, she was not to leave her bunk, which meant that she had to eat the prepackaged MREs because she couldn't join us in the dining hall. Anyone who's ever had one knows that was probably the cruelest part.

The next day, I brought her back a cup of ice cream from the mess hall. It had melted into chocolate soup in the Kuwaiti sun, but she appreciated the gesture nonetheless.

"I'm sorry I didn't tell you about him. We –"

I cut her off.

"Don't mention it."

Neither of us needed the extra drama right now. Focus.

***

Everyone had been buzzing about how "American" Arafjan was. I decided to take a walk to clear my mind and find out for myself. Just a stone's throw away from our living quarters was a Baskin Robbins, a Chinese restaurant, a short-order Burger King, a Pizza Hut, and a barber shop. If this is war, I think I might stay awhile! All that was nice, but the most beautiful thing about Kuwait was that all the fighting was on the other side of the border.

Troops from all around the world came and went – Canada, Spain, South Korea, Estonia, Albania, the U.K., and Australia. But not us; we enjoyed the amenities for two more months. The reason we stayed so long was because we were such a small group that it was hard to place us. We would have to be attached to a larger division but most didn't need extra logisticians; they had their own. Then one afternoon full of thumb-twiddling, Captain Johnson burst through the door panting and out of breath. "Vacation is over, we're going to Iraq!"

CHAPTER 11

Rumors were swirling about how we got here. Our executive officer, Lieutenant Miller, revealed that Captain Johnson told the big brass at Arafjan that we wanted to leave! This was largely erroneous. I mean, we came here to do our part and we wanted to be productive, but ONLY when we had a mission. Until then, sharpening our card-playing skills was fine with us.

Questions began to arise. "Where exactly are we going with no mission? Where exactly are we going, period?!"

The most we could hope for was that we weren't being put into a hot zone unnecessarily because our "fearless leader" was growing impatient. We loaded up our two Hummers and rolled out. I remember buying some cheap portable speakers and jimmy-rigging them to our truck. We bumped 50 Cent's first two CDs on repeat to keep ourselves amped up and I could probably still recite every lyric right now if you asked me to. His song that proclaims "Many men wish death upon me" took on new meaning, mainly because it was accurate as hell. It's strange to think that someone woke up today with a very short to-do list: "Kill an American."

As we continued north over the border, we each took turns sitting in the back with the one M249 SAW machine gun we were issued. Peering through the sights from the perched seat and swinging the turret from left to right, I felt less and less like Movement Control and more like somebody who could possibly be forced to take a life.

Our new orders had us driving to the closest post of "friendlies" in Southern Iraq, the HQ for the British Army.

"What's our ETA in Basra," I asked curiously.

"A little over 2 hours. Sit back and enjoy the ride."

"Easy for you to say; you're not manning the SAW!"

We were very susceptible at this point because we had no heavy artillery and even if we did, lest we forget, we were still just 12 people in unarmored trucks. A mortar would have torn through us like paper Mache. The first crackles of gunfire in the distance are something that sticks in my head like a Post-It note. It was hard to gauge how far away it was and even harder not to play out all the scenarios in which you could die.

To make it worse, the desert night has a funny way of playing tricks on both your eyes and mind. You think you see movement where you didn't, think you heard sounds where there weren't.

"Just get through the night, Kristian," I sighed to myself.

As the sun crested over the hills the next morning, we pulled into camp. I checked for vipers, scorpions, and camel spiders, none of which make great cuddle buddies, before taking a nap underneath my Hummer, the only place I could find shade.

Little "luxuries" we had been afforded in Kuwait, like running water, all but vanished since entering the combat arena. There were no showers and no restrooms, at least not one you'd expect to find in America. We were mandated to stay within Army grooming regs but, without a faucet to run your razor blade under, shaving quickly rose to number one on my list of least favorite things to do. What water we did have was rationed daily: three canteens and not a drop more. Drinking two a day kept the dehydration away; the third I generally used for bathing.

But we had bigger issues than dry shaving. The Brits had no missions for us. They told us we could stay as long as we needed but suggested we'd find more luck further north. After about a week of hustling the U.K. boys at Spades, we shuffled back into our Hummers and motored to An-Nasiriyah and Imam-Ali Air Force Base.

An-Nasiriyah is the birthplace of the Bible's Abraham. For a history freak like me, walking through a scene out of the book of Genesis is probably one of the coolest things I've ever done. Aside from that though, the former Iraqi air base could have doubled as a tourist attraction for a different reason: it must have been "The world's biggest junkyard." There were scraps of old MIG fighter jets everywhere. They were all in various stages of decay, but even the most intact ones didn't look like they would have been fit to fight in their heyday. After commenting on this to an Iraqi National, he explained that they were cheaply built in Yugoslavia and that Saddam had chosen to spend less money on military equipment so he could keep more for himself.

Tucked away in the westernmost corner of Ali, we assembled a large hoop tent in the dry clay under our boots. A cot to sleep on was a welcome change from the warm sand under the truck. There was no floor to this tent, and we were often woken up to the sounds of one of the girls screaming because a snake or a scorpion had crept in overnight. I was usually tasked with disposing of whatever caused the disturbance because, ever since that elephant at Disneyland, handling animals has never bothered me, and I'd have happily done that all day over what we did next.

We were still orphans without a job and once the command got word of a bunch of "squatters," they took full advantage and gave us the worst duty imaginable. See, there were these huge metal drums all over the compound that were used as latrines and that waste had to go somewhere. I'll give you three guesses who had to take care of it and the first two don't count! We'd drive around post all day with JP-8 gasoline in tow and, whenever we'd see one of those metal drums, we'd have to douse it with fuel and set the human waste on fire. Once ablaze, it had to be stirred like beef stew, with a stick, until

87

it dissolved and evaporated. Ain't that some s***? I'm a believer that everyone's role is important, but I would have rather found another way to contribute.

While at Imam-Ali, it came time to re-up on our anthrax and malaria shots and Sergeant Christopher Beach, who was directly above me, asked me to transport our medical records. Call me nosy, but on the drive over, I peeked into Captain Johnson's file. Turns out, she lied to us and our families before we left. THIS was her first time in-country! The fabricated tale she spun about serving during Desert Storm? Turns out she sent care packages TO those serving in Desert Storm from a very safe Fort Lee, Virginia. She knew just as much about surviving in the field as the rest of us. I'm all for keeping morale high – which is why I didn't say anything about the secret I uncovered – but don't feed everyone what you think they want to hear to give us this false sense of security. The higher-ups thought it would be best to split the "dirty dozen" into two groups of six, hoping it might be easier to place us this way. I was in the six that stayed while the other half went to work the airport in Baghdad. Sidney was in that group and even though we hadn't spoken much since Kuwait, I was bummed to see her go. There wasn't much action to report in An-Nasiriyah except that we were always stirring up some s***, literally.

10 weeks later, we were ordered north too and arrived safely in Baghdad, which was a miracle in and of itself. The Baghdad airport

and its surrounding area were worse than Chicago, DC, and Detroit combined. It was where the most ticks on the death toll were added at the time, easily making this the most dangerous part of the trip. Fortunately, we were allowed to tag along with a convoy of Marines for protection because I'm sure our one Hummer would have looked like a pretty sweet target chugging along by itself. There were several times they had to disembark from their vehicles and return fire. They were an actual infantry squad, so we were told to just hold tight and let them do what "Devil Dogs" do! I know Soldiers and Marines talk a lot of smack to each other over whose branch is better, but I'm greatly indebted to the USMC. They've saved my ass more times than any soldier would like to admit. The pings and pangs of the barrage of bullets whizzing by were close enough to see their ricochets but we managed to get inside of the wire. Once inside, we learned that the rest of our team had been sent even further north, so they found odd jobs for us like counting pallets and shipping containers and placing ID tags on them.

Boom. Boom. Boom. You couldn't even brew a cup of coffee without a mortar round making contact outside the gates and even if you did, you certainly didn't have time to drink it. I don't think I've ever slept less in my entire life. The scariest part is that you don't know which rocket, if any, has you marked and it's not like you can fire back to protect yourself. Your only line of defense is to pray that the next incoming one doesn't have your name on it. You're 6,934 miles from home, in 100+ degree heat, with 50 pounds of gear on your back and someone actively trying to kill you, and you STILL have a job to do. It's trippy.

A few months had passed when our tour of Iraq moved on to Kirkuk. Still no sign of our other half, but those who were permanently stationed there told us that they had been by.

"Sounds like they're having just as much luck as we are," said Lieutenant Miller. "There's only one other place I can think of."

Camp Diamondback in Mosul is the northernmost part of Iraq occupied by Americans. Mosul is a major city with homes built into the shelves of a mountainside. The Army base was on the plain below, which gave the insurgents a sort of bird's-eye vantage point if they shot from the hills adjacent to us. Lieutenant Miller was right. It was there we found the missing six.

CHAPTER 12

It was so good to see some familiar faces, particularly Sidney's. Our time apart had made me forget about the snafu with her fiancé and actually brought us closer. She told me our team had grown quite the reputation with the big wigs at Diamondback, and not in a good way. They thought it was time to "call an audible."

Instead of making us all relocate like everyone else had done prior, they promoted our executive officer to commander and sent Captain Johnson to Baghdad to work at the airport without us. Under new leadership, we were attached to the Screaming Eagles of the 101st Airborne Division out of Fort Campbell, Kentucky. This was a huge honor because the Screaming Eagles are one of the most celebrated and legendary units in U.S. Army history. We called an "audible" too and voted on the idea of living in separate tents, away from the higher-ups. Now, the newly-christened Captain Miller and the Non Commissioned Officers would have their own space, and the other seven of us would have ours. We were assured that we would be here in Mosul for the duration of our deployment and we could settle in and start to get comfortable – well, as comfortable as you can be with a bounty on your head. For the first time, despite being at a war where 125,000 lives were lost (total, Coalition and Enemy), there was a small part of Iraq that felt like home.

The rainy season of Northern Iraq swooped in and flooded our entire tent from the ground up. We got smart though, using scrap lumber to build a floor, just elevated enough to keep the water underneath it. We figured with 7 months left, we might as well make the place a bit more inhabitable. We got thin rope and strung it along the ceiling of our tent-like clothes lines to section off our own private areas, then we used bed sheets to create walls between us. I took the corner closest to the door, which prompted Sidney to take the spot right next to mine. I found that if I pulled the tent stake closest to my "room" out a bit further, it looked the same from the outside, but dramatically increased my living space on the inside. I like to see myself as a visionary. I took one look at the new dimensions, and nothing but possibilities danced in my eyes. "I'll transform these extra cubic feet into a penthouse!" I got resourceful, going to the supply guys and cutting a deal with them to get an extra cot. I tied both of my cots together and placed a sheet of plywood on top to eliminate the curvature in the middle and make it flat. The next time we went out into the city, I did a little shopping. I picked up a mattress and two pillows and a couple of bed sheets to boot. DaVinci's Masterpiece was the Mona Lisa; mine was a queen-sized bed during a war!

As movement control, we worked cooperatively with Iraqi Nationals on a daily basis. Because we were in such close proximity, they would be searched for weapons before entering the perimeter. This was a little worrisome for us because, while they were mostly trustworthy, they were privy to seeing Diamondback's layout. They knew where the hospital, dining hall, motor pool, air hangar, and other strategic targets were and, once outside of the wire, you just never know who they'd be talking to or drawing maps for. We'd get their trucks fueled, document their cargo, tag it, and then give them directions to a drop-off point. Every now and then, you had a little skirmish with a driver about the MP unit assigned to protect them on their trip, driving faster than they could keep up with. Although they were Iraqi, just like the factions who were attacking us, they too often feared for their lives. Working for Americans makes you just as good of a kill as being American.

The power would be on the fritz regularly so to prevent being bored silly without TV, we'd play soccer with the Iraqi drivers. They told us stories in their best broken English of what it was like to live there – horrifying accounts of merciless torture and murder performed by Saddam and his cohorts. How if the national soccer team played poorly, he would take them out back and shoot them like wounded dogs. They were literally playing for their lives. Looking at their pain-filled faces as they hung their heads, it was hard not to feel for them. We were doing such a good job with the Nationals that our one-year tour got extended for six more months! If this was a reward for a job well done, a pat on the back would have sufficed for me. Please don't misunderstand me; I was ecstatic that we finally had a mission, but keeping us those six months longer than planned means 182 more days and an infinite amount more chances for the enemy to kill you. I knew we had been there too long when our routine mortar attacks would whistle through the camp and everyone stopped running for cover. After a while, you resign yourself to the acceptance that today may very well be your last day on earth and there's nothing you can do about it.

I resolved to make the best of it, but there were times when tempers ran as high as the temperature. I recall one afternoon in particular – ironic because it was so hot – when I lost my cool. Each unit was rationed a block of ice per day. It was my one day off for the week, my team was behind schedule at work, and I decided to do them a favor by grabbing the ice for them. When I got to the big freezer, the line was a mile long if it was an inch. I took my place at the back and patiently waited. Sergeant Beach, who didn't know I was already there, pulled up and spotted me in the crowd.

"How long you been waiting," he asked.

"Around 20 minutes," I replied.

"The water in the tent is hot enough to make coffee as is, and the faster we can get the ice, the better," he said.

"Agreed," I said, nodding.

He leaned into me and whispered, "How about you be a team player and fake an emergency to get to the front of the line?"

My eyebrows furrowed in disbelief of what I was hearing.

"Sarge?...I..."

"You heard me, Aleixo,"" he said firmly, his tone sharp as a ginsu. "Don't make me repeat myself."

"That wouldn't be fair to the other soldiers. They've been waiting on this line just as long as I have, some even longer in the same 105-degree heat," I tried to reason.

His eyes locked onto mine like a homing missile.

"You disobeying a direct order?"

"It wouldn't be right," I said, shaking my head in disapproval.

"I am the sergeant here and you are not."

"But unfair is unfair," I insisted.

"I didn't ask for your philosophy on ethics. You're disobeying a direct order and that is subject to punishment."

By this time, our oh-so-healthy conversation had caught the attention of others in line.

"Stand at parade rest when you talk to me, Specialist, as a sign of respect," he demanded.

When I didn't do that either, he placed his hand on my shoulder and I brushed it away... "respectfully."

"Unless you want a bigger problem, you'd refrain from doing that again, Sergeant," I said, trying my best to maintain some semblance of military etiquette.

"Is that a threat," he asked, his nostrils flaring inches from mine, close enough for me to hear his inhale.

"Why don't you come find out?" One thing about me is that I do not fold when I'm asked to do something I don't believe in. He unhooked the clasp of the M249 SAW from across his chest and I undid the velcro on my flak jacket. We squared up, taking defensive stances as I glared at him over the tops of my knuckles. Everyone in line was shouting for us to calm down, but we were well past that being an option. Our feet shuffled in the Mosul sand, trading hooks and jabs. He landed a shot just under my right eye that left a subsequent shiner but missed with a follow-up haymaker. I charged at him, teeth clenched, and connected with an uppercut to his chin, splitting his lip. Me with an eye swollen half-shut, him spitting blood, we left it all out there. As we tumbled under the desert sun, the post Command Sergeant Major was called over to break it up. I thought I was in major trouble but, after he heard what started the bout, he told me that he would've done the same thing and I was off the hook.

I needed a vacation, bad. With our tour now extended, we were each given slots to take leave for 2 weeks but, because we were such a small unit, there were only two to go back to the States. We voted unanimously to give those to Sidney and one other girl who also had a daughter. The rest of us had to either go to a retreat in Dohuk – a small holiday town in Kurdistan, renowned by troops for it's um... "working girls" – or barter a flight out. I had made fast friends with one of the civilian chefs that cooked for us. He was taking his leave at the same time and invited me to the Mull of Kintyre Music Festival in his home country of Scotland. "I'm down but I ain't wearing a kilt!" While awaiting a connecting flight to Glasgow, I saw a gang of military pilots at an airport bar. I couldn't hear what their conversation was about, but I could feel their aura. These were men of danger, the most skilled of their breed and certainly the most fearless. I couldn't tear my eyes away from their brown leather jackets, and it wasn't just the bomber designs that caught my attention. Patches adorning the breast pockets of the cowhide, symbolizing all the countries they had flown over and all of the missions they had executed, I found myself in both awe and admiration. In that moment, I had a new vision. I needed to become one of them; I needed to become a combat pilot.

***

The next "fortnite," as the Scottish would call it, was a blur, and the R&R was over just as quickly as it started. Stepping off the plane back in Iraq via Kuwait, I was eager to put the rest of this deployment to rest. My welcoming party? The sound of magazines being emptied and roadside bombs detonating. The defining moment of the last leg of this nightmare was this one morning that I can still see now if I close my eyes tight enough. I physically get sick to my stomach thinking about it.

Rocket-propelled grenades were launched all the time from the hills above our base. On this early morning in particular – the one I don't like to talk about – the blasts were louder than usual.

Midnight. Boom.

1 A.M. Boom.

2 A.M. Boom.

Closer...closer.

"It's about time they hit something. They've been practicing long enough," we joked.

Our immediate thought was that someone was trying to nail the fuel station. One good shot there would turn the whole camp into a scene out of *Backdraft*. And then, silence.

I couldn't fall back to sleep in the eerie quiet, tossing one way and turning the other. Restless, I got dressed early and showed up to my shift before my scheduled time. As I walked into the motor pool, the sun was just coming into view. The pastel-colored sky was deceptive, its beauty masking the truth of what occurred the night before. I was greeted by solemn faces.

"What's up, guys? Don't tell me Captain Johnson is back," I remarked playfully.

That's when I heard it, heard *him*. There was uncontrollable sobbing coming from the fence that separated Diamondback from the neighboring civilian farm. It was the Farm's owner. The RPGs that hit overnight had killed all of his livestock and crops. All of them.

His entire field was littered with the bodies of his cows, horses and chickens; nothing had survived. His own countrymen had mistakenly done this to him.

I walked to the fence and curled my fingers around the links. He was on his knees, weeping and as he looked up from the dirt and our eyes met. His expression seemed to beg the question, "Why?"

I didn't have an answer for him and that brought tears of my own. There was nothing I could do for him in that moment except cry with him. He was a living casualty, and there have been very few moments in my life where I've been sorrier than I was for that man. The tour dragged on for a few more months, but took on a different meaning in that it took on no meaning at all. I had come here to prove something to myself and I wasn't sure what that was anymore. I mean, I like to think that I did some good. But who knows?

"Orders are in! Pack your things. Wheels up at 0800, we're going back to the U.S. of A.," Captain Miller announced, waving the paperwork in his hand. Everyone chanted "Home, home, home, home!" But all I could think of was what if "home" isn't an actual physical place? What if home is a state of mind, a peace of mind? In that regard, I couldn't go home if I wanted to; I had seen too much. On our way south to Kuwait, the plan was to stop at the airport in Baghdad and pick up Captain Johnson. Although she had been separated from us for the majority of the mission, we came as a unit and should leave as one. All 12 of us, the "Dirty Dozen." You can imagine our shock when we got there and were told she left months ago.

WHAT?! She didn't even say anything!

We had a 2 week layover in Sevilla, Spain at Moron Air Force Base, which served as a great place to try and decompress. When we got stateside, we exited the terminal to find Captain Johnson waiting for us with the families.

"All safe and sound, Kristian," she asked, wearing the most plastic smile I'd ever seen not on a mannequin. She deserved an Oscar for her performance that afternoon. I couldn't even look her in the eye. We had a ceremony at Gate 12 of "incoming flights" at Sky Harbor International Airport, where I was promoted from specialist to Sergeant and given my Global War on Terrorism ribbon and an Army

Commendation Medal. Six months overdue, this was supposed to be a joyous day, but as I looked around and saw everyone hugging their families, I couldn't help but notice that someone was missing.

My father.

I blamed myself for my own disappointment. It wasn't his fault for being absent, it was my fault for thinking he'd be anyone but himself, even on this day. He didn't teach me how to drive, how to shave, how to ask a girl for her phone number, or how to tie a tie. So why would he be here now?

CHAPTER 13

Although I didn't have blood relatives to pick me up, my buddy Keith and three friends from my church were there to greet me. As we caught up in the car on the long haul home from Phoenix to Tacoma, Keith told me he and the crew were leaving the next night for Outer Banks, North Carolina. They had rented a beach house for 8 days and asked if I would like to come. Frankly, I had enough sun where I just came from to last me a lifetime, but the thought of alternatively spending that time with my dad and step-mom kinda made the decision for me. I stuffed a few tank tops, printed shorts and my flip flops into a duffel bag and met them at Keith's. With everyone taking turns driving, we arrived in OBX in 3 days flat. I had never been to a beach house before and, after 18 months of desert living, the seagulls and smell of salt water were more than welcome. The doorbell rang a half hour later, but I wasn't expecting company. I swung open the squeaky screen door to find four girls standing there, beach towels and boogie boards in hand. I guess the fellas failed to mention that we'd have guests. I kept peeking at their sedan in the driveway, halfway hopeful that there was a fifth girl hiding in the back seat for me("You can come out now!").

There wasn't. But you know what? I was cool with being the 9th wheel. I wanted to be around friends, but I also needed space to myself. I spent all my sunrises and most sunsets on that beach, collecting shells, watching the waves pound the shoreline, and reflecting.

One night, the air got too crisp for me out there, so I packed it in. All the couples had gone to the inlet to eat and I had the place to myself – a perfect opportunity to throw a few logs into the fireplace and stretch out in the La-Z-Boy recliner. While watching the flames crackle, my peripheral vision caught a glimpse of a book on the cedar coffee table. It belonged to the owner of the house. I didn't know it then, but that book was about to change my life. It was *Wild at Heart* by John Eldredge. It didn't have a golden glow radiating around it like you'd see in a comic book, but it was almost like I was meant to find it. At a time when I was confused, lost, and unsure about the next phase of my life, it provided some much needed insight. I couldn't put it down for the remainder of my time at the beach house. The plan to live my life for the foreseeable future had begun. In fact, when we got back to mainland North Carolina, the first thing I did was stop at a Barnes & Noble to buy a copy of my own. That book became the father I never had. The father I needed.

Somewhere in rural Kentucky, I split from the guys on their way west. I had an itch to visit Allentown, Pennsylvania to see a good friend – Sidney. I know our romantic involvement was to end with our time in Iraq, but I had 3 weeks left of vacation to kill and Tacoma would only remind of me how I just survived 547 days at war and my dad wasn't the first person to hug me when I got back.

We spent the next few weeks discussing our individual futures and recounting our top 10 stories from the deployment.

"I'm thinking about becoming a combat pilot, you know," I said smugly, impressed with my own decision.

"Why am I not surprised," she replied, shaking her head.

Looking out the window of seat 17C on the flight back to Arizona, I had just one thing on my mind: becoming a chopper pilot. When I got back to post, I made it priority #1 to express my interest to my superiors. They put together my commission packet and submitted me for the position. Several interviews and close to 14 weeks later, I arrived home one evening to find a white envelope from the review board on my door mat. I slowly peeled open the flap, hoping for good news on the inside. YES! I had aced the selection process and was approved to attend the Warrant Officer Basic Course. All I had to do now was pass the physical, which shouldn't be a problem for an athlete like me, I thought, and I'd be given a date to attend school.

Two days later, enter Amy, a fellow soldier from the Intelligence Division and a friend of a friend. It was nearing the end of the work day and a buddy named Daryl suggested we go to a pub. I don't drink, but I'm always up to hang with good company. Amy had overheard Daryl and I making plans and invited herself to tag along. "I thought you said she was Intelligence? What's she doing hanging out with you," I joked. He had known her for a few months and insisted that she was cool, so I didn't have any objections – although my agreeability may have been swayed by her honey-brown eyes. Amy and I playfully bantered all night over games of darts, some of which I even let her win. Daryl told us we could crash at his place since he lived nearby and it was getting late. But there was no crashing. Despite having an early morning the next day, we stayed up like two children on Christmas Eve. I didn't need her distracting me from my pre-course studying but, from then on, you never needed GPS to find either one of us; we were always with each other. We planned to keep it that way. That is, until I was given orders to return to Iraq.

It was a highly inconvenient time to say the least; not that going to war is ever "convenient." I was a Warrant Officer Candidate now and in a serious relationship; I didn't want a deployment jeopardizing either one of those. I was just there 13 months ago, but it felt like 13 days ago and here they are, sending me back? I was outraged but my rage and $1.50 would get me on the bus. This time was considerably more difficult than the first because I didn't volunteer and it came complete with a very emotional goodbye to Amy. Between her and pending Warrant Officer School, I actually had a reason to want to stay home now. I was assured that this tour wouldn't affect my status as a Candidate; it would just be as simple as rescheduling my course date when I got back. That is, if I got back.

And, like the sequel to a bad blockbuster, I returned to Northern Iraq. The only solace I took was in knowing that Captain Johnson wasn't my Commander and I knew somewhat what to expect. I reprised my role as support to the 101st Airborne Division and helped launch what would become the largest railroad operation in a foreign country since World War II. I think the crucial work I was doing as an honorary Screaming Eagle was how I managed to stay sane this time around. Days were spent outside of the wire on the gritty, sewage-ridden streets of the cities where anything could happen. I'm talking "full flak jacket, 8 thirty round magazines of 5.56 caliber rounds and my gas mask" anything can happen! The railroad we built delivered vital supplies and became the glue that held about 30% of the overall mission together.

Each track we laid down translated into more lives saved – Iraqi *and* American.

The nights were for burning through phone cards calling Amy. Usually just a lot of telling her about the logistics for the trains but I remember one time in particular, I had a more interesting story to share. We were trotting through a town near Tikrit, overseeing the construction of some fresh tracks and every time we'd stop, the local children would run up to us and ask for money. One dollar was like a winning lottery stub to them. At a point, I parted with my last single and when I told this little girl, who couldn't have been more than six years old, that I didn't have any more cash, she chucked a Snapple bottle full of urine at me and stuck up her middle finger. That was it for me. I was desperately ready to stop playing "Rambo" and go home.

About three months until the completion of my tour, I was sitting in our Sunday chaplain's meeting, kind of like church, when my mouth got drier than toast. We kept a lot of Gatorade with us and I kept drinking them, trying to shake my thirst. Still, somehow the cotton-mouth just wouldn't go away. Naturally, I had to use the bathroom more frequently, which I attributed to the increase in my Gatorade intake. Standing up for what was probably going to be my 3rd bathroom break of the hour, my vision became blurry like a camera out of focus and then...THUD! Lights out. When I came to, I had Daryl rush me to the camp doctor. I told him my symptoms and he had a suspicion that made him immediately request a blood test. I was asked to stay overnight and I couldn't figure out why. I just knew it must be serious if he wanted to keep me. The next morning, he swung the makeshift curtain surrounding my bed open.

"I've reviewed your results and it seems conclusive that you are in the early stages of diabetes. Do you have a family history of it?"

My heart sank like a penny in a glass of water. My mind instantly flashed back to that Christmas, the card, the teddy bear...my mother in the hospital.

"Yes sir, my mom died from it."

"Your glucose levels are over 900. I'm amazed that you're still actually able to stand."

"I'm glad I could impress you," I thought to myself sarcastically.

He dropped his clipboard on the bedside table and reached out his palm.

"I'll be needing your weapon."

My eyes began to quiver as my rifle exchanged hands, and I was trying my hardest to fight the tears that wanted to fall. He patted me on the back and walked out of the room. The second he was out of view, I wept. Not cried, but wept.

12 hours later, sitting there in the medical tent, I could hear the mortars whistling like tea kettles overhead and I didn't even care. I had seen how quickly diabetes stole my mother and I had so many questions, not for the doctor but for God. Why me? Does this mean I'll be dead soon? *How do I live now?*

Sleep eluded me that night. I was too preoccupied with my emotional pendulum swinging from "completely numb" to "massive depression."

The following day I asked the doctor for insight into how this could have happened. He explained to me that I was born with the gene and it stayed dormant. I had a 1 in 10 chance of it being activated, although he suspected that if it were going to be activated, it would have been much later in life, like my mid-forties or fifties. He mentioned that high amounts of stress have been linked to jump starting the dormant genes for chronic illnesses, though.

Check!

There aren't too many things I can think of more stressful than war. He informed me that I would be getting Medivaced to the big hospital in Stuttgart, Germany for further stabilization. Everyone wished me luck but I'd need more than that.

It took 2 weeks as a lab rat and a barrage of tests and different medications to get my sugar level consistently under control. I was counseled for depression and educated on the new dietary rules I had to abide by, along with being taught how to inject myself with a syringe of insulin 4 times a day. I was then given the option of going home to America or finishing out the tour. I didn't hesitate.

"Send me back in, sir," left my lips faster than a jackrabbit can run. "My unit and I came together and we WILL leave together." All I could think of was that if I let diabetes take me out of the game now, who knows when it'll stop. In my mind, I couldn't let it win. Not this round, not ANY round.

CHAPTER 14

Much to my comrades' surprise, I returned to the battlefield.

"Don't tell me I have to get my own bags, too," I quipped as I slid out of the back seat of the Humvee. They shook their heads in disbelief. Many said that if they were in my boots and were given an out they would have taken it. I guess that's where we're a little different. No matter the situation, if faced with a choice, I will always choose to fight. My superiors welcomed me back but put me on light duty, per doctor's orders. I protested and told them that I could manage but was quickly reminded that it wasn't up for debate. There was a lot of down time for me after that. Too much, maybe. If I hadn't come to terms with mortality yet, being at war with a disease made for damn certain I did now. Coming to grips with the knowledge that I would be sick every day until I die was staggering. I can't even trust my own body not to turn on me.

The only thing that kept my inertia moving in a forward direction was the prospect of becoming a combat pilot in just a few short months.

But those months crept by at a snail's pace. Finally, with the railroad 3/4 of the way complete, we handed the baton to the Iraqi Nationals to finish it off, and I had earned my 2nd Army

Commendation Medal in the process. It was time to go back stateside and reclaim some sense of normality – a real house to sleep in with a real bed and a caring girlfriend to be supportive. With my new physical challenges stacking up like a game of Jenga, I spent my month off restructuring my life. Except, I had no clue how much restructuring I was about to do.

My first day back at work, I was called into my Commander's office, presumably to tell me he'd heard about my diagnosis on tour. I was right – but that wasn't all he had to say.

"They won't let you fly."

"Why not, sir," I asked, baffled by the news. "I worked very hard and passed all the tests."

"The sole limiting factor at this point is your health," he replied matter-of-factly.

"My health? With all due respect sir, that's B.S. and you know it! My hands and eyes work just fine. It's just my pancreas and you don't fly with your pancreas!"

"I know, I know. I understand," he said, motioning with his hands for me to calm down. "But this is coming from the United States Army, not me. If you want things changed, you'll have to go in front of the Medical Review Board. Until then, you're on light duty."

It's like they were punishing me, as if diabetes wasn't punishment enough. Because I was a Sergeant, they put me in charge of the post flag detail. I was responsible for making sure the ten soldiers they gave me – an assorted bunch of others with their own bag of medical issues – reported on time and raised the flag at 0500. We would take it back down again at 1700, combining for a literal 20 minutes of work a day. During the 12 hours in between, I'd mess around with computerized flight simulators and combat air strike video games, still keeping the faith that the Medical Review Board would change their initial ruling.

I had researched what questions they'd ask and rehearsed my answers in the mirror for weeks in preparation. My goal was to know their protocol better than they did and find loopholes in their argument. It took a few months to get a date, but my "big day" before the MRB finally came. The review took 72 hours to complete. I passed everything with flying colors – except for the blood test. My hemoglobin A1C was at 12 (very high). When the dust settled, I wasn't just told that I couldn't be a pilot anymore, but that if I were to stay in the Army, I'd have to reclass to another job because of Movement Control's likelihood of being deployed. I asked what I'd be re-classing to and tried my best not to cringe when I heard 42 Lima – Administrative Specialist. While I believe that every job is essential, I didn't come here to sit behind a desk and file papers. I came here to live out an adventure. I came here to feed that kid who'd ride a skateboard through an intersection just for the rush of it. You already took my dream from me. I'm not going to let you CHANGE it for me too!

I chose to be medically discharged and take my chances on the outside. The Board gave me a release date set for 6 weeks out and told me I would be receiving a severance check. It was the 13th day of February in the new year when I buttoned that camouflage top for the very last time. I caught a bittersweet reflection in the mirror. "Aleixo" stitched above one breast pocket, "U.S. Army" above the other, the 101st Airborne Screaming Eagle on my right shoulder, American flag on top of it.

Whoa, that was me!

The Army had been my ticket out of Tacoma and a way to see the world, but it had also been where I met my greatest enemy: diabetes, the thing that stole my mother and my dream. I had no Plan B, or any other letter in the alphabet for that matter. The military had become such an extension of me that I struggled to find an identity without it. Since escaping Iraq the second time, I had already been a bit out of it, but THIS took me so far out of it, that "it" became just a dot on the skyline. I was so numb that I never felt hungry or tired. I'm sure I was a terrible boyfriend to Amy at this point as well, because I wouldn't open up about anything either. My bedroom became my fortress and I barricaded myself in it. Looking back, the word "Serendipity" springs to mind. It's my favorite word in the English language – a fortunate,

113

unexpected happening. My vision was clouded by depression so I couldn't see it then, but my discharge was, indeed, a positive thing.

After moving out of the post barracks, I was in my new studio apartment unpacking a cardboard box that I hadn't touched in ages. Near the bottom, I found an old autocross magazine, frayed and ripped at the edges. For nostalgia's sake, I combed through it, some of the pages sticking together. Towards the back, there was an ad for a high-profile sports car racing series. I stared at the page so long, the images became like 3D.

"What if I...?"

With every bit of urgency that you would expect from a man who just lost his life's ambition, I took to the internet, scouring for any information I could possibly find on the series. Obsessively, from the second my eyes opened to the rare occasions that they closed, I was in pursuit of details on the sport. I knew all of the drivers, teams, cars, and their specs, but one question still remained...

How do I get in?

I mean, I knew autocross like a fish knows swimming, but that's different. The most damage you can do there is kill a traffic cone! I learned that I needed to attend a specialized school to achieve a racing license. Some were as expensive as $20,000, and even the cheap ones would set you back a few grand. With no substantial money until my severance check popped up in the mailbox, I had to play to my strengths and get resourceful. I got a hold of the series sanctioning body's personnel directory. Listed inside were the names and email addresses of all the race directors in all 50 states – easily a thousand or more. I began emailing each one individually and asking if they'd be willing to lend their tutelage and mentor me on how to drive a real race car. In my mind, money, or lack thereof, had not only built a door around racing, but it had locked me out, and these emails would be the key back in.

Clickety-clack.

I sat in my swivel chair typing into the graveyard hours of every night. I'd type until my brain quit on me and I'd fall asleep on the desk, wake up with drool on the keyboard, and start all over again the next day. Amy would try to get me to go outside and relax, but for what? The sun and fresh air were stupid; this was all that mattered. If she didn't bring me food every now and again, I'm certain I would have starved to death! For me, passion was nourishment enough. I'd survive off that.

As the responses came rolling back, I was tempted only to get discouraged. They were all negative. I had a mountain of replies thanking me for contacting them and wishing me the best of luck but ultimately ending with the line, "Sorry, I can't help you." Some were even a bit more creative. You'd be surprised how many different ways people can tell you "No." To be honest though, I couldn't blame them. This is the world's most expensive sport and I probably wouldn't let some kid who had only ever done autocross drive my expensive race car either. I became immune to it. "No" doesn't mean I can't do it at all; it just means I can't do it with you, now. You can reject me all you want. It will not change my course of action. It took weeks, but I hit "send" until there was no one left on the list.

Ping!

My computer alerted me to a Gmail chat request. A gentleman who ran a sprawling, 12-turn road course out west had written me. I clicked the envelope icon with bated breath. Was it another "no" to add to my collection?

The message was simple. Just one line.

"How bad do you want it?"

I asked myself the same question. Was I delusional from losing my career and clinging to a fantasy of turning an old hobby into a full time job, or did I really want it as bad as I thought?

I typed back.

"Very much so," sat on the screen for a moment while I gathered my thoughts before finally pressing "Enter."

"Prove it...where do you live?" was his response.

I told him Arizona and he replied with, "Great. I'm in southern California and it should only take you 18 hours to get to me. If you're as serious as you say you are, you've got 24 hours to get here."

Whoa. After pinching myself, I put Google Maps into the search bar. "Leaving Cochise County," read the sign as I hit the freeway in the middle of the night. My white '95 Ford Thunderbird had close to 300,000 miles on it and a tendency to overheat. I had to calculate stopping every four hours to let the engine breathe and add coolant to my travel time, but I made it.

My tires slowed to the 10 miles per hour recommended by the yellow placard on the gated entrance of Coastal Raceway. A security guard with keys jingling from his side pocket leaned into the driver's side window.

"You need help?"

"I'm here to see the boss."

He directed me where to park before escorting me into the race control tower. There were offices at the top and my eyes were greeted with a hawk's view of the track.

I waited. I wanted to pace the floor because that's what I do when I'm in heavy thought. I was guessing at all the questions he would ask and what my responses would be. The glass door marked "CEO" swung open and there stood the man who had challenged me to the trek. 5 foot 9, medium build, dusty brown hair, and all the permanent forehead wrinkles of a thinking man. I shook his hand firmly.

"Don Allen. I see you took me up on my challenge."

"How could I pass it up," I answered confidently.

"I'm semi-impressed. Please, have a seat," he said, offering a large burgundy leather chair directly in front of his desk. The office was spacious, with a 20-foot ceiling and wall-to-wall carpeting swallowed my feet with every step. Meticulously placed racing trophies sat in the glass displays behind his desk and race win clippings from magazines and newspapers were stacked just as neatly in front of those. He locked his fingers together and stared at me.

"Kristian, how long is a minute," he asked.

I almost chuckled at the simplicity of the question but caught myself, figuring it was some sort of test.

"60 seconds?"

"Is that a long time?"

"No sir, not at all."

His eyes widened with shock.

"Oh, really?"

This made me nervous. Had I said something wrong?

He pointed to a clock on the wall.

"Tell me when a minute goes by starting..." *Tick, tick, tick.*
"Now!"

As I watched the second hand begin its lap around the face of the clock, he sprung from his seat and buzzed around the office like a chainsaw, organizing papers, making a cup of coffee and even a phone call! Someone at the front desk chimed in and confirmed his order for lunch. When the minute was over, he sat down, kicked up his heels and crossed his legs along the ridge of the desk.

"Still think a minute isn't a long time?"

Naturally, I changed my answer.

"First rule of racing: every second counts," he said.

He asked me to ponder how much he could have done with 2 minutes, 5 minutes, or 10. He made it sound possible to take over the world if he had an hour! He reached into a desk drawer and pulled out a huge binder, so full that the pages were threatening to spill from the spine. His coffee mug shook when he dropped the binder on the table.

"This is a to-do list, and if you're going to work here –"

"Wait, work here?"

"How fast do you think you can get all of this done," he asked, pointing at the contents.

"Just give me a deadline, sir, and I'll make it happen."

Don laughed.

"I like your enthusiasm." He wagged his finger at me. "That's the attitude you're going to need to have. What are your goals?"

I told him my story and that I wanted to learn to race, trying my best not to sound as desperate as I really was. We got some fresh air as he gave me a walking tour of the facility. We stopped on the opposite side of the paddock at garage number four and he slowly rolled up the gate as if unveiling a secret treasure. I peeked inside. There, on blocks, was an old road race prepped '87 Datsun 280ZX. He made me a deal.

"If from 6 A.M. to 5 P.M. every day, you chip away at this to-do list for me, and then when we have some free time in the evenings, we'll take the Datsun out and I'll teach you how to drive it – I mean really drive it."

He made it clear, however, that this was going to pay in experience and experience only. No money.

"That's fine. I think I have enough in my bank account to get me by until my severance check comes," I said. That wasn't entirely true but it got me the "job."

We shook hands as I thanked him for the opportunity and I was told I would start on Monday, just two days away.

The 18 hour drive back to Arizona, still making stops every four hours along the way, gave me plenty of time to mull over my decision. I absolutely, unequivocally, undoubtedly had to move to California on Monday. When I got home, Amy asked how it went. I was excited to tell her, but hesitant at the same time; I didn't know how it would affect our relationship. I paused, took a deep breath and told her everything. She asked if I was going to go and if so, what about our plans for the future.

"Do I fit in them," she asked.

"Did she," I thought.

Honestly, I had been so focused on the opportunity that I hadn't really factored her into the equation.

"It's a job that doesn't even pay, Kristian," she shouted, her frustration peaking.

She told me that it would be stupid of me to go, that I didn't know what was out there or if this would work out at all. She explained that what we had was a sure thing and I shouldn't give that up to chase after something uncertain. She told me that long-distance relationships never work out for her and if I left, we would be no exception. I didn't want to break her heart. I couldn't even say anything because I knew that, if I uttered one word, she'd start crying, and I didn't want to risk changing my mind.

As we stood there in silence, she could tell the cement around my decision was quickly drying. I went to the bedroom and started packing while her sobbing echoed in the hallway behind me. Zipping my last suitcase, I heard "This doesn't make any sense" from around the corner.

"It doesn't have to make sense to you. I love you, but it makes sense to me and that's all that matters." It crushed me to say that.

We talked that night about everything. It reminded me of the first night we met. Love stories don't always have a happy ending and if I didn't go, I would resent her and we'd both be miserable. She said she felt like leaving her behind was less important than my dream, and she was right. I was thinking of myself and well, it was about time I did. My life had been dictated by a series of circumstances that I had no control over until now, and here was my chance to take it all back.

Sunday night came and she asked me to reconsider one last time. We shared a final kiss. I thanked her for everything, slung my bags in the trunk of the T-Bird, and watched her disappear in the rear view mirror.

CHAPTER 15

I was wide awake when I hit the freeway on-ramp. My windows were down and I was trying to catch the faintest of breezes on an otherwise muggy evening. I imagined the humidity and brief spurts of cooler, passing air to be symbolic of life – mostly thick enough to suffocate but here and there, you're given a breeze. I had to hold onto my breeze. I kept my foot on the gas all night and, as I crossed the border into California the next morning, I remember rounding the bend of a single lane stretch of road, glancing to my left, and seeing the bluest water below the reddest mountainside. It was mesmerizing. The sun shimmered on the waves and, in that moment, I knew I had made the right decision.

I was back at Coastal Raceway, but I still needed a place to stay. I knew I wouldn't have been able to afford much on my razor-thin budget and was disappointed to see that even the most meager of rooms was still out of my price range. Sure, my severance check was on its way but, with no income, I'd probably need that money for food and gas. I knew of only one place that was easy on the wallet and always had a vacancy sign up: my T-Bird. I parked in the rear of the track's lot. It was hidden from the office's view by the grand stands, so Don couldn't see that I was living out of spot 419B. If it got too chilly at night, I'd curl up in the backseat but, most times, I'd throw on an old purple University of Washington Huskies sweatshirt and sleep on the roof. There was very little ambient light and I could watch the shooting stars put on a show from up there. It was a little reminiscent of being back in Iraq.

Most people would have high-tailed it back to their comfort zones at the thought of no phone, no internet, no TV, no house, and no family, but without sacrifice there can be no reward. I just broke up with my girlfriend of 2 years to pursue this dream and I couldn't turn back now, no matter how hard it got. I don't come from a wealthy family who could pay for my racing, my last name isn't Earnhardt or Andretti, and this may be the only chance I get to make it happen. Ironically to my benefit, this wasn't a foreign concept. I had been homeless for much of high school and thrived when there was nothing to thrive on. At least this time I didn't have to sneak past security guards and keep absolutely still for fear of setting off the motion detectors. Come to think of it, I was also homeless for a lot of that first tour in Iraq, too. No showering out of a canteen here, though; there was a big wooden box, like you'd find at the beach, with running water overhead. At 5:00 A.M., I'd begin my day by evicting these tiny tree frogs that crept in through the shower window and clung to the walls. By 6, I was dressed and cleaning out the garage stalls for renters. 9 sharp was when the boss liked his coffee: "Macchiato, blonde and sweet like my wife," he'd always say. Then we'd go over the track agenda and what needed to be done for the day. Next, I'd go out into the Golden State sun, beads of sweat already forming above my lip, and begin to mow the close to four mile long lawn. A track of this immense size needs just as much maintenance as you think it would. I never had much of a "Green thumb," but there were a lot of weeds to be tended to along the fence line and grass that had to be seeded and watered as well. When I wasn't a landscaper, there was just as much painting to do. The start/finish line and the yellow edges around the apron could always do with a few strokes of a brush. Other days, I was a salesman with a phone to my ear, cold calling companies to see if they'd like to advertise with a banner by the tire barriers or perhaps the track newsletter. Then I'd drive into town and deliver said newsletters to all the local businesses.

Weekends, when we'd have a race or an HPDE (High Performance Driving Education) event, I'd wish I was an octopus. I'd start off as gate security, then jump on concessions, peddling popcorn, hot dogs, burgers, water, and soda before moving to the merchandise trailer to sell hats, t-shirts, hoodies, and polos. I never minded, though. It was a privilege to be that close to the cars and I love the smell of octane in the morning!

125

When I was off the clock, Don and I began to cultivate a friendship. On Fridays, he would take me to a local short track 30 minutes outside of town to watch the asphalt sprint cars and midgets shred around the oval. We'd place $1 bets with each other on which driver would take the checkered flag. His guy would win nine times out of ten but, because he knew my pockets weren't deep, he'd tell me he'd put it on a tab and I could pay him when I got rich. We weren't there for the gambling though; we were there for the rumble of the engines, the sound of tires screeching, the heat from the stadium lights – we were there for the experience.

On my favorite nights, the ones when he had time and just before the sun said adieu for the day, he'd play Mr. Miyagi to my Daniel-San and teach me how to drive. The first time in the Datsun was a disaster. All these gauges and buttons, I couldn't even start the damn thing! The learning curve was steep because I didn't have a karting background. Yeah, I'd done autocross, but these weren't orange cones and this wasn't my grandfather's Beetle. The throttle would go all the way to the floor and want to stick like it had gum behind it.

Turns 1-5: "What the HELL am I doing?"

Turns 6-12: "I'm actually doing it!"

Slicing through the wind, I knew that nothing could touch me, not my problems, not my past. When you're at this kind of speed, the only thing that can catch you is death. The human body is fragile and we've been taught to respect it but, when you're in a race car, I like to think that death has a little respect for you. You're challenging it, daring it, laughing in its face and, if you're lucky, you may even get to walk away from it in the end. Whatever I went in search of in the Iraqi desert when I volunteered all those years ago, I had just found.

I spent over 365 nights on the roof of that car and about half as many evenings trying to make every lap faster than the last. I'm a visual person and I work best by memorizing landmarks.

See that sign? Apex now.

See that tree? Brake late here.

I ran it until I was making turns almost involuntarily. It wasn't an easy year for me. A little, well a lot lonely, but the best educations aren't born from comfort and seldom do they come when you're in a crowd. With no money, I had struggled my way into sitting behind the wheel of a racecar and logged enough hours for my first competition license. Although I still had so far to go, this was an accomplishment I could hang my hat – err, helmet on.

More than a year later, I had eaten through most of my severance money – literally! Meals weren't free, even though I was eating as little as I could and testing my body to see how long I could go without a bite. I wasn't sure how much longer I could go on without a bank deposit and I prayed I didn't have to find out. Someone upstairs heard me.

One Saturday afternoon, a Formula BMW driving school from up north rented our facility. They were regulars here and the director, Steve Tolbert, and I got to talking. He knew of my "unpaid internship" and inquired about how I was doing financially.

"Unless there's some secret trust fund or a dying rich uncle who's left me in his will that I don't know about, I don't know what I'm going to do."

By conversation's end, he had offered me a job at his private school, part-time in the office and part-time on track as an instructor. His 11th-hour heroics not only brought a paycheck but, even more valuable than that, I wouldn't have to sacrifice any seat time. I was sad to leave my then-mentor Don but, fiscally, I just couldn't stretch it any longer. I thanked him for his time and leadership and told him that what he had done for me meant the world. All you need is ONE "yes," and he was it. As my Thunderbird made its way out of the gate at the 10 miles per hour prescribed by the yellow placard, he posed the question he had asked in his first message.

"Hey, Kristian."

"Yeah, Don?"

"How bad do you want it?" His usually stern face broke into a smile.

And with that, I was on I-5 North, headed towards The Bay. I worked at Steve's school for about 8 months when I was introduced to a prominent businessman. He had just purchased a new set of wheels that made me wonder when NASA started making cars, and he came to take Steve for a joyride. I poked around with my new boss to see how he could afford it.

"Oh, Mr. Monopoly? He owns one of just about every restaurant chain from here to Mexico."

The food service industry was where he made quite a living, but racing sports cars was his real passion. I saw him several times after that – always in a new car, always flashier than the last. I mean, the guy had a serious passion for one-upping himself! It wasn't until he unloaded a Porsche 911 GT3 from his '53 foot Feather-lite trailer for Steve to check the springs on that I decided to chat him up. The car itself was probably the least expensive I'd seen him with, but that wasn't what raised my eyebrow. The sticker plastered on the windshield was the insignia of one of the premier sports car racing series in North America.

"Are you a driver?"

"How fast do you go?"

"Ever been in a wreck?"

I had four cups of coffee that morning and was firing off questions like a Gatling gun. I think it may have been my over-caffeinated enthusiasm that impressed him. I didn't know the first step of getting onto a race team when I asked him about an open position. He said they had a vacant Test Driver seat but I probably wouldn't be interested because they were based all the way in Buford, Georgia, near Road Atlanta.

In his defense, he didn't know me very well.

Hell, I'd move to the moon if that's what it took.

"Georgia, eh," I said, rubbing the hair on my chin while I thought. "I like peaches." Steve told him my driving was still raw but I had promise.

We walked away with a "gentleman's agreement" until his attorneys could send me the proper paperwork. The ink on the contract hadn't even dried before my bags were packed.

"Now boarding: Flight 373. SFO to Hartsfield-Jackson Airport."

CHAPTER 16

To the layman, the role of Test Driver is comparable to that of a Triple-A ball player. You're in the farm system just waiting for your chance to be called up to the majors. I was honored just to be here, just to have a spot on the team, just to zip up the same fire suit as guys with three times the experience. Most had been karting since they could walk, so I beat on my craft every day to compensate for my relatively late start. If the veteran drivers slept in, I got up. If they went to the gym at 5, I got there at 4. If they left at 8, I stayed till 9. There wasn't a single driver who made less money than me, but I worked like I was their marquee guy. I treated that season of club-level racing like it was the Monaco Grand Prix and, on the 1st day of July, square in the middle of the schedule; I shot out of the final turn at Mid-South Motor Sports Park and hoisted my first trophy as a race winner! There was no champagne and no fireworks, but in my heart, the whole city had thrown a parade.

My day to swing a bat in the majors with this team never came, but while with them at Sebring International Raceway in Florida, a chance encounter in the paddock netted me some solid advice. Walking back to our hauler – and admittedly looking down at my phone and not where I was going – I literally ran into a very well established race/stunt driver who was cleaning his helmet. He had been a hero of mine since he appeared, arms folded, on the cover of my first sports car racing magazine. You likely wouldn't know him by name but you've undoubtedly seen his work. If I named all the car commercials he's done "donuts" in, you'd be like, "Oh, *that* guy!"

After picking my chin up off the ground, I found him very friendly and easy to talk to. Despite becoming star struck and fumbling over a couple of words, I managed to ask a few questions. I wanted to know all about his story and how he got to where he was. I went into mental stenographer mode and probed for step-by-step details. He put down the wax-soaked cloth he was using to buff out the scuff marks and explained that his path in professional motor sports and mine cannot be the same. It was a different era when he came up and, while funding was still a factor, it didn't make or break a guy.

"There were no agents. There were no pay-to-play drivers. The fastest man got the seat. If an owner wanted you, he wanted YOU. It was because he knew you could win and not because you brought a check that looked like a phone number."

He also let me in on the lesser-known fact that most of his checks got signed by a popular auto manufacturer for doing those wicked commercials. If this were the DTM series in Europe or the V8 Super Cars in Australia, where sports car racing is more appreciated by the mass consumers, he might be able to live off of his base salary and purses, but it'd be tricky to do here in the States.

"Ovals. If you're looking to line your pockets doing this, you might want to try this little bush league called NASCAR – I think they're going to be big," he said with playful sarcasm.

"Probably not what you thought you'd hear from me, but just something to think about if you don't get 'the call' from your team. Anyway, I've got to run. Good meeting you."

"Thanks. You too," I said, waving as he walked off.

Hmmm...NASCAR?

For the rest of the week, I rooted my team on in practice and qualifying from our pit-stall and gained valuable knowledge from shadowing our engineers. Race day came and we were fraught with electrical issues. Although our drivers finished well below what we had hoped, in P11, I left with a spiral pad spilling with notes. "Being behind THAT wheel right there is what they're grooming me for," I thought, placing both palms on the hood of the still-warm car. The dream was so close I could tangibly reach out and touch it. I just have to get 'the call.' But what if I don't get 'the call?'

That evening, while grabbing a cheeseburger at a local dive named Sammy's, I had my focus stolen. The thief in question was a golden-skinned waitress with eyes as sweet as licorice. Sebring is a race town and she could tell I wasn't a native.

KRISTIAN ALEIXO & BRAXTON A. COSBY

"Racer," she asked.

"Yeah, kind of."

"What hotel are you staying at," she quizzed, collecting my money for the bill.

"The Doubletree on Circle Drive. Why?"

"You're cute. I can't promise I won't stop by later."

"I didn't realize Sammy's made house calls. I'm in room 108, but I can't promise I'll let you in," I said, trying my best to play hard-to-get as I left a tip and exited.

There isn't much to see in Sebring aside from its historic race circuit, but my waitress made sure I saw a lot of her for what was left of the weekend. I even missed my ride to the airport and, ultimately, the flight back to Atlanta with the team because I was having so much fun. I tell that story in the interest of keeping this book "real," but also as a warning to the younger male readers. Having to reschedule my flight was a minor infraction, and having to pay for the flight out of pocket was a moderate inconvenience, but under different circumstances, the consequences could've been more costly. Distractions are omnipresent and can shape shift. Sometimes it's a pretty girl, other times it may be partying, drugs, or alcohol. But if you work tirelessly and sacrifice greatly like I did, then you can't let it be in vain. I'm not in the business of losing – not to anything or anyone – and I vowed never to lose focus like that again.

Back in Buford, I stirred on the advice that one of my idols had given me. After careful deliberation and being partially spurred by his words, I announced that I would not be renewing my contract option at the end of the season. Being a Test Driver was momentarily pacifying but, in my mind, waiting for a team's current "Golden Boy" to vacate his ride, be dropped by a sponsor, or (God forbid) get injured was leaving too much to chance. The $40K a year I made was a far cry from the goose egg I'd earned at Coastal – and Lord knows I would've done it for free. But my future family can't eat ambitions, and they can't wear my aspirations to stay warm in the winter – I learned that from my dad. No, if my future family was going to be founded on my passion, I'd have to create something.

With ovals still fresh on my brain, I took a risk and bet on myself. I'd start at the bottom and climb the rungs to a six figure income. I looked into a program designed to generate more racial and gender minority participation in the sport. I reached out to some of the participants but got a hodgepodge of reviews, some very negative. I don't put much stock into hearsay and I believe that everyone should base their conclusions on their own experiences; I just didn't have an expendable year or two to throw away forming my own. I entered the NASCAR Whelen All-American Series as an independent. There were more pay-to-play opportunities here than ever, with an emphasis on the pay part and no drought of teams that would readily let me run their cars as long as the check cleared. Nobody at this level could afford to let me do it for free, much less pay me for it. On the track, it's a given that at some point you will hit a wall. Off the track, it's a given that, at some point, money will be a wall. For the next two seasons, I bounced around the mini and street stock divisions like a pinball, shelling out my own cash to whatever owner needed someone to cover his next tire bill. I kept the lights in my apartment off, even at night, just to scrape up enough to get back in the seat. We'd run, trade more paint than stock shares in Sherwin-Williams, and it'd be back to 17th-century living until I could do it again. But discomfort is nothing when your dream is staring you in the face. How much am I willing to bleed for this? Dry! This is the only way I knew how to gain ground on those born into more fortunate situations. With the testing and races I could afford being few and far between, I pushed myself twice as hard. The rest of these guys would be back out here next weekend, but I wouldn't, so I had to make every lap count.

While counting my pennies, I got word of a competition for qualified drivers. The prize was a one-year contract with a NASCAR Camping World Truck Series team. A chance to go 3 wide with the likes of Sauter, Crafton, and Hornaday sounded a lot like the call I never got as a Test Driver. The goal was to raise as much money as possible in a four-month time frame, and whoever raked in the most sponsor dollars at the end would get the ride. Most guys crowd-sourced their family and friends. Me? I tried to "Captain Ahab" a corporate whale. I'd craftily camp out in company lobbies and chase CEOs to their cars – anything to get them to meet with me. I managed to finagle a breakfast date with an energy gum company from the Czech Republic. They very expressly gave me 20 minutes and I made my pitch over eggs, bacon, and coffee in their hotel restaurant. Their accents were difficult to understand and their faces even harder to read. As the marketing director guided his cup of espresso back to its coaster on the table, he motioned for his associate to hand him a manila folder. Inside was a blank check on which he wrote "$20,000!" That was more than I asked for and definitely enough to keep the other drivers off my back. Meanwhile, the team was in talks with a propane company that was founded by a retired Command Sergeant Major (U.S. Army) who was keen on war veterans and wanted to contribute to my efforts.

"Now, I know it's not much in your sport, but would $950,000 help you out, young man?"

The room spun. After all the times I've cried, been on the verge of giving up and broken my own back, here was a company willing to invest almost a million dollars in me. Regrettably, internal operation issues forced that Truck Series team to close its doors before we could make good use of the funding and I had to give the money back. I was both devastated and thankful. Although we were unsuccessful, it was a privilege just to be in the position to lose a million dollars. I wholeheartedly hate losing but this proved I belong in those six-figure conversations and that someone thinks I'm worth all that money on a racetrack. And you know what? So do I.

EPILOGUE

I was taking a breather to re-strategize my approach to NASCAR when a random phone call from a buddy who had known me since my racing infancy called. He invited me to the Circuit de Navarra in Arcos, Spain to test for Team USA in the Formula Car World Series. He had already secured a seat and thought I'd be a good add-on.

"What do you say, Kristian? I need someone to block for me."

"Block for you? That'd be kinda hard from in front of you!"

"Smart ass."

I hung up the phone, flattered to be invited to represent America in a foreign racing series going for a World Championship. The last time my feet were on Spanish soil, I was returning home from an 18-month nightmare in Iraq. This time, they were resting on the brake and throttle of a 600hp, Ferrari-built space ship. With my visor shut and peering out over the missile shaped nose, I swept through the 15-turn road course. My confidence swelled, listening to the team engineer chirp lap times in my ear with every passing of the start/finish line.

"2 seconds off the pace."

"1 second off."

"Half a second under."

I'm still working on being a road course ace, but I had rattled off some solid laps – enough for them to offer me the ride. Unfortunately, we weren't able to lock down a sponsor in time, but it got me thinking about formula cars again. I had really enjoyed my days at Steve's school with some of the Formula BMWs that we had. The NASCAR stuff had given me a deep appreciation for oval racing and that's when I had an epiphany. Why not marry the two? Formula cars ON ovals. There's only one sanctioning body that does that: IndyCar.

I've since set my crosshairs on the six ovals (Phoenix, Indianapolis, Texas, Iowa, Pocono, and Gateway) of the 17-race Verizon IndyCar Series schedule. The biggest, the granddaddy of all the races on that schedule was, of course, the Indy 500. It's arguably the most prestigious race on the planet, and I need to experience it from the cockpit at least once in my life. There are steps to getting there, though; you don't just get on the court with Michael Jordan because you think you can hoop. I must start on the "Mazda Road to Indy," IndyCar's official ladder system, in a USF2000 car. There are only 2 rungs from there that separate me from etching my name in the history books forever. My driver coach, a former 500 driver himself, advised me that an asphalt midget car would be an optimal starting point when building up to eventually turning left at 230 mph. So in transition to open wheel, I spent all of 2015 testing and racing a winged one against some of the kings of the northeast: guys with 10-20 years of experience on me. This, too, was on my own dime and made possible through a dedicated diet of ramen noodles and so many peanut butter sandwiches that I should be sponsored by Skippy! Midget cars are a kick because they're so challenging to wrangle in. They're featherweight machines with enough horsepower for a car twice its size and, because of the insane power-to-weight ratio, it doesn't take much to get one airborne. The car was demanding, but I'd say overall it was a successful year with a bunch of top tens, a couple of top fives, and a best finish of fourth, just one shy of the podium. The only spill that had me questioning my future eligibility for life insurance was at that track in Pennsylvania, where I had my rear clipped by the car behind me before getting plowed into and snapping four ribs like pencils. Too dumb to stay down, I cut the typical 3-4 week recovery time to 11 days when I took to the iconic 18-degree banked half mile oval at Nashville Fairground Speedway a week and a half later. Despite the physical pain, I had a good showing. Trouble with the brake bias during qualifying was like salt to a slug and meant I had to charge from the tail of the field. I overtook a few cars and got about mid-pack before a car spun in front of me and became an unavoidable target.

On December 31st, 2015, while everyone I knew was preparing for the night's festivities, I was loading the last of my cardboard boxes into a U-Haul bound for the racing capital of the world: Indianapolis, Indiana. My New Year's resolution? Get closer to the sport and begin my training.

The so-called "realists" will tell you it's too hard. They'll ask, "Why don't you quit?" They'll say, "You have a chronic disease, your last name isn't Andretti, you don't have a rich daddy, you haven't been go-karting since the age of five, and most of the guys out there don't even look like you. You have every disadvantage in the book and no one would blame you if you just quit." I'm the underdog of underdogs, but THAT is what makes this the outside groove. My answer to them is simply "I can't" I've lost good women, my sanity, and way too much money. I take four injections in the abdomen a day to stay alive for this and this alone. I've sacrificed everything and given my whole heart. If I gave up now, what would it have all been for? Besides, racing gave me an escape from a life I didn't want and created the one I did. And one day, racing will give me everything my father couldn't, and things I've never even dreamed of. A driver is compelled to chase the thing in front of him and I'm chasing immortality. This story ends with plenty of room for the next, to tell you about how I overcame even more odds and started – possibly even won – the Indy 500. Maybe I'll quit then.

Maybe...

SPECIAL THANKS

Sometimes, the best dreams are the ones you didn't even know you had. This book is proof. This book is *My* book. Still surreal to say and I don't think I'll ever get used to it. The life I was given would have crushed the will of the less determined but I always fought back. As challenging as it's been, it's given me a story. I'm ever grateful to the Cosby family for the opportunity to tell it and for the chance, through my words, to live forever. My appreciation doesn't end there though...

To my mother, Madeleina: If life was that wallpaper, you were always the brightest cloud of them all.
Eu vou te amar para sempre.

To Mr. Sackeyfio: What is a man? Someone who can only become one when another, like yourself, believes in him. You had all the ingredients and told me I did too. Thank you for being the first.

To Johan Sandqvist: My viking friend. We don't share a single drop of blood but surely, you are my brother.

To Keith March: Whatever relationship I've had, have or will ever have with my Lord and Savior, Jesus the Christ, is because of you.

Special thanks to:

Don, Hudson, Brian, Blu, Gene, Kenny, Michael, Todd, Danny, Kevin and anyone else who has ever strapped me into their race car.

Joe Beckham and Hector Scarano (iHeartRacing), Darren Mix (Race For Veterans), Todd Knaparek (Bydand Graphic Solutions) and Kelly Jones (RaceCraft1) for partnering with me on my quest for the 500 and even more so for your friendship. I don't know how you 5 put up with me sometimes.

Lastly, my supporters and anyone who has ever offered an encouraging word! You've pushed me on days when I didn't think I had anymore to give. When I finally do take the green flag at the Indy 500, it will be just as much because of you, as anyone!

ABOUT THE AUTHOR

Iraq War Veteran and 2 time U.S. Army Commendation Medal recipient for meritorious achievement, Kristian Aleixo, is a gambler. Once a highly regarded combat helicopter pilot prospect, his ambitions of flying an AH-64 Apache onto the battlefield were shattered with a diagnosis of Type 1 diabetes while on tour in Iraq. With his new chronic illness, this gambler bet on himself, using the same hand-eye coordination and reflexes that would have made him a pilot, to chase down his teenage dream of being a professional race car driver. Without a name like Andretti or karting experience in adolescence, he's had to risk more than most to sit at this table. He's moved cross- country on a whim, been homeless and done everything but file for bankruptcy to keep moving forward. Through resourcefulness and tremendous sacrifice, Kristian now finds himself as not only a driver but a budding author and an avid humanitarian. He regularly volunteers with homeless children and adults as well as multiple children's hospitals, and his goal for the near future is to found an organization for kids with diseases, like himself, who aspire to be professional athletes. Any gambler will tell you, there will be more losses than anything. The good ones will tell you, the trick is to keep playing until you've got the perfect hand, bet huge and that one win will trump everything that came before it. Kristian Aleixo is *that* gambler.

Follow Kristian @

Twitter:

@kristhebullet

Facebook:

www.facebook.com/Kristian-Aleixo

www.facebook.com/kristianaleixoracing

ABOUT THE AUTHOR

Bestselling Author, Braxton A. Cosby is a dreamer who transitioned his ideas on pen and paper to pixels and keyboards. He tells stories that evoke emotion and stimulate thought. Braxton is a multi-award-winning author who has penned all kinds of genres from health and wellness, science, dystopian, and superhero fiction, as well as autobiographies from the likes of many movers and shakers in the industry. His Amazon Bestselling *My Life In Story Series* with Mike Clemons and three time Olympic Gold Medalist Gail Devers is a passion project that he's forever grateful to be a part of. His new superhero adventure book, THE CAPE is book three of the Dark Spores Series. He is the CEO of Cosby Media Productions and lives in Georgia with his amazing wife and highly energetic Morkie named StarKozy.

Follow Braxton @

Websites:

www.braxtoncosby.com

www.cosbymediaproductions.com

Twitter: @BraxtonACosby

Facebook: www.facebook.com/BraxtonACosby

ENDORSEMENTS

Special Thanks To These Supporters

MORE BOOKS FROM

THE MY LIFE IN STORY SERIES

MIKE CLEMONS: MY LIFE IN STORY

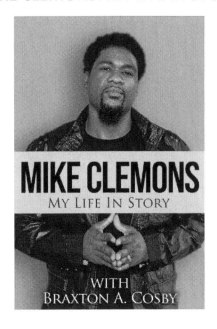

GAIL DEVERS: STRONGER

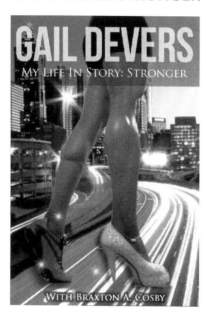

Cosby Media Productions

Entertaining the Mind, and Inspiring the Soul

www.cosbymediaproductions.com

Made in the USA
Columbia, SC
20 October 2023

24316378R00091